THE USE OF THE SCRIPTURES IN COUNSELING

JAY E. ADAMS

First Orthodox
Presbyterian Church
Sunnyvale, CA

BAKER BOOK HOUSE
Grand Rapids, Michigan

PHOTOLITHOPRINTED BY CUSHING - MALLOY, INC.
ANN ARBOR, MICHIGAN, UNITED STATES OF AMERICA
1975

CONTENTS

PREFACE

I send forth this volume in the hope that it will help many both as a stimulus and as a guide in the work of biblical counseling. Varied forces are at work today to pry Christians loose from a biblical base. Some claim that the Bible cannot be used as a textbook for counseling, and that any attempt to do so violates its purpose and plan. Others maintain that we have not become biblical enough. Although this volume does not answer such critics directly (see my book *Your Place in the Counseling Revolution* for a fuller discussion of this matter), nothing could serve as a more powerful refutation than to set forth successfully a positive biblical perspective and methodology as I have tried to do here. I shall allow the reader to judge for himself whether, indeed, I have succeeded. This book, together with its practical outworkings in *The Christian Counselor's Manual,* while (obviously) quite imperfect, I think that you will agree, nevertheless plainly shows that biblical counseling not only can be, but is a reality. May this volume contribute to reaching an understanding of those guidelines that are needed to help pastors and other Christian counselors keep from wandering off of the narrow way that (unfortunately) so many have found too strait for their liking.

Jay E. Adams
Westminster Seminary
Philadelphia, Pa.
1975

INTRODUCTION

The controlling design of this book is to be as concrete, informative, and practical as possible. Yet there is at the outset a certain amount of foundational work that must be done in order to support the more concrete structures that I hope to build. So, let us break the ground and pour the footing.

CHAPTER I
Christian Counseling Is Scriptural[1]

You Must Use the Scriptures in Counseling

I do not think that I need to labor this point at Dallas Seminary. I am sure that the reason why I was invited to deliver these lectures in the first place was because of our common conviction about this vital imperative.[2] Therefore, since I think that I can safely assume that we are in basic agreement about this, since I have argued the issue elsewhere in print[3] and since I am certain that your interest lies more in questions growing out of problems connected with the ways and means of using the Scriptures in counseling, I shall quickly move beyond this point. But before I do, perhaps a word or two would be in order.

You Must Have Conviction, Courage and a Steady Determination to Use the Scriptures in Counseling

First, you may think that it will be easy to graduate from this school, take up your work in a conservative pastorate, and as a part of your effort there, begin to do biblical counseling. Please believe me when I say that it will not be that simple. The pressures exerted against a ministry of biblical counseling are great, as you will discover all too soon. For one thing, when you begin to

---

[1]The first eight chapters of this book were given as the W. H. Griffith Thomas Memorial Lectures at Dallas Theological Seminary, November 6-9, 1973. Subsequently, they were published in the four issues of *Bibliotheca Sacra* during the year 1973. They have been revised and additional chapters have been included for use in this volume.

[2]I have retained much of the original lecture flavor in these chapters.

[3]Jay Adams, *The Christian Counselor's Manual*, pp. 92-97.

1

counsel biblically some counselees will rebel. They will protest that you are being unduly hard on them, and will demand an easier way out. After all, scriptural counsel is often *hard.* Sin creates no *easy* problems; they are all so difficult that it took nothing less than the death of Christ to meet them. Untangling men from the webs of sin can be a quite painful process. The hard (but needed) directions that you will give to others from God's Word about repentance, confession of sin, reconciliation with one's brother, and so on, will not sit right with those who want to remove the miseries caused by sin without dealing with the sin itself. Though men want it, you must tell them that there is no such instant holiness.

Second, because sinners (and never forget that *Christians* are sinners, too) always want to do things the easy way,[4] they often will insist on bypassing the hard work of determining from the Scriptures what God's solutions to their problems may be. Instead, they will run to faith healers, exorcists, and those who claim to receive extra-biblical guidance or revelation for quick answers; they will plead experience as the interpreter of the Scriptures[5] or will try to use the Bible as a talisman from which to extract magical answers. For instance, more than once parents will appear for counseling dragging their rebellious teenager, whom they have failed to discipline for the past seventeen years, and say (in effect), "OK, do it to him." They expect the counselor to put two feathers in his hair, do a short rain dance, wave the Bible over the boy's head seven times and pronounce him "cured." Such people are not happy when they learn that they may have to spend from six to eight weeks establishing Christian communication and developing biblical relationships with their son. They wanted a

[4] That is one major reason why people get into trouble in the first place and find it necessary to seek counseling.

[5] A very prevalent problem in our irrational day.

medicine man, not a Christian counselor. To resist these tendencies and instead hold out for careful exegesis and application will not always be easy.

Third, you will find too that even in the midst of the present disillusionments with it, many Americans still worship science—and science falsely so-called. How else could B. F. Skinner, who pontificates that man is merely an animal, and that the world's problems can be solved by scientific retraining, command such a large hearing today? Members of your congregation, elders, deacons, and fellow ministers (not to speak of Christians who are psychiatrists and psychologists) may turn on the pressure and try to dissuade you from any resolute determination to make your counseling wholly scriptural. They may insist that you cannot use the Bible as a textbook for counseling, try to shame you into thinking that seminary has inadequately trained you for the work, tempt you to buy all sorts of shiny psychological wares to use as adjuncts to the Bible, and generally demand that you abandon what they may imply or openly state to be an arrogant, insular, and hopelessly inadequate basis for counseling. They may even warn and threaten, as they caricature the biblical method: "Think of the harm that you may do by simply handing out Bible verses like prescriptions and pills."

All these—and a dozen more—pressures will be exerted upon you to give up any idea of a scripturally founded and functioning system of counseling. Combined with personal doubts that may arise during times of discouragement, these pressures can be greater than you now may think.

What then can be done to meet and to resist effectively all such pressures? There is but one answer: during periods of pressure look to the Scriptures for their help in doing this too. The counselor's Counselor is the Holy

3

Spirit, speaking by His Word. All of which leads us to an examination of the important question:

What Does Scriptural Counseling Involve?

Your encouragement and assurance will come from an understanding of this matter. The answer to the question is that counseling that is truly scriptural is (1) motivated by the Scriptures, (2) founded presuppositionally upon the Scriptures, (3) structured by the goals and objectives of the Scriptures, and (4) developed systematically in terms of the practices and principles modeled and enjoined in the Scriptures. To put it simply, scriptural counseling is counseling that is *wholly* scriptural. The Christian counselor uses the Scriptures as the sole guide for both counselor and counselee. He rejects eclecticism. He refuses to mix man's ideas with God's. Like every faithful preacher of the Word, he acknowledges the Scriptures to be the only source of divine authority and, therefore, judges all other matters by the teaching of the Scriptures.

In short, such counseling takes the Scriptures seriously when they say that they are able to make the man of God[6] "adequate," and equip him for "every good work."[7] In the passage from which those words come, Paul piled words and phrases upon one another to convey the idea of *complete adequacy:* the Scriptures not only make the Christian minister "adequate" for his work, but, as Paul put it, "entirely equip him for it." Not only do they thoroughly anticipate and show him how to meet all possible pastoral counseling situations, but by doing so they make him adequate (Paul insisted) "for *every*"—not

---

[6]In the pastorals this designation, picked up from the Old Testament, is used for the Christian minister. Cf. I Timothy 6:1. See also Deut. 33:1; Josh. 14:6; I Sam 9:6; I Kings 17:18,24; II Kings 1:10,12; 4:7; 5:8.

[7]II Timothy 3:17.

4

just for some but—*"every* good work" that his office requires of him. Because the minister, *par excellence,* must counsel as part of his life calling,[8] he knows, therefore, that God's written Word will adequately equip him for this phase of ministerial work. While all sorts of other resources may be useful illustratively and in other secondary ways, the basic principles for the practice of counseling are *all* given in the Bible. Counseling that relies upon these principles is scriptural. This leads us to the main matter before us:

The Use of the Scriptures in Counseling
*The Scriptures are the Counselor's
Textbook for Counseling*

Like his Lord—who was the wonderful Counselor predicted by Isaiah—the counselor will find that all that he needs for the work of counseling is in the Bible. Jesus Christ needed no other text to become the world's only perfect Counselor. He was that because He used the Scriptures more fully than anyone else either before or since. His counsel was perfect because it was *wholly* scriptural in the absolute sense of those words. The minister who engages in scriptural counseling, like Him, believes that because the Holy Spirit inspired the Book for that purpose, the Bible *must* be used in counseling.

Arguments that one does not use the Bible as a textbook for architecture or for mechanical drawing beg the question. If God has assigned the task of nouthetic confrontation to ministers as part of their life calling[9] and He has given the Scriptures to them to equip them fully

---

[8] For the argumentation behind this assertion see Jay E. Adams, *Competent to Counsel,* pp. 42ff. and *The Christian Counselor's Manual,* pp. 93-95.

[9] See argumentation for this in Adams, *Competent to Counsel,* pp. 42ff.; *The Christian Counselor's Manual,* pp. 93-95.

for this life calling, then it follows that the Scriptures, while treating other matters as well, adequately furnish all that ministers need to counsel. Remember, the Scriptures do not purport to give shipbuilders or architects or electrical engineers detailed information for pursuing their arts, but they *do* claim to equip ministers adequately for theirs. Indeed, where else may one turn to obtain the precise data needed to meet the two major issues in counseling: namely, the problem of how to love God and the problem of how to love one's neighbor? After all, we spend little time discussing counselee problems about things; it is in relationships with God and with other persons that counseling problems develop. The Scriptures, in *focusing* upon these two questions, provide "all things" pertaining to and necessary for "life and godliness." With Martin Lloyd-Jones, the Christian counselor affirms, ". . .every conceivable view of life and of men is invariably dealt with somewhere or another in the Scriptures."[10] When it comes to counseling, then, eclecticism is not an option. The issue resolves itself quite simply into this: if a principle is new to or different from those that are advocated in the Scriptures, it is wrong; if it is not, it is unnecessary.

It is at this point that so many of the self-styled professionals balk. They want the Bible in part, but not *solely,* as the basis for their counseling. Yet, just because of the fundamental nature of the question, it is right here that one makes the most vital decision about counseling; it is here that he decides whether his counseling will be wholly scriptural (and, therefore, Christian), or whether it will be something else.

---

[10]Martin Lloyd-Jones, *Truth Unchanged, Unchanging* (New York, 1955), p. 16.

*The Scriptures Tell the Counselor All That He Needs
to Know About God, His Neighbor, Himself
and the Relationships Between These*

They speak of man's nature, as a creature who bears God's image and likeness, his basic problem (sin) and God's solution in Christ. They tell him what counseling should be, provide the content (i.e., the counsel) for it, detail the qualifications required of those who do it, and govern and regulate the methodology that may be used in it. What more is needed? Apart from the Bible, who else has such information?

You Must See Scriptural Counseling Alone As Adequate To Meet Man's Problems

All right, we have generalized enough. *How* does this all come out in the wash? *What* does scriptural counseling mean in concrete contexts? Let us conclude this article with some examples of scriptural counseling that will serve to point up more vividly what I have been saying.

Start with the most difficult counseling problem of all: death. To be more specific, let us ask who best counsels a grief-stricken widow following the death of her husband? Who is adequate for this task? Is the psychiatrist? The clinical psychologist? You know that he is not; and so does he. Quite seriously, what does he have to offer? On the other hand, are you competent? Armed with God's scriptural promises you *know* that you are adequate. You know that among God's children you *can* (as Paul put it) "comfort one another" with God's words (1 Thess. 4:18); you know that God has said that the scriptural data in 1 Thessalonians 4 will act as an anchor for the believer to keep his grief from drifting into despair, and that they will moderate that grief by balancing it with hope, so that in the end, through scriptural counsel the widow is enabled

7

to sorrow in a way different from others "who have no hope" (1 Thess. 4:13).[11] And to the surviving one who does not know Christ, in that hour the only word that can make any real difference is the redemptive word of the gospel, by which, in God's providence, the Christian counselor may be used to bring eternal life to her out of the occasion of death. If the Christian counselor can handle the most serious counseling problem adequately, there should be reason to suppose that he can handle others that pose less difficulty too.

"Not fair," I can almost *hear* someone say. "You've stacked the deck in your favor; everyone knows that death (at least until recently) has been the peculiar province of pastors." While I do not think that it is at all unfair to begin with life's most difficult counseling problem, since it so clearly points up the contrast between psychiatric inadequacy and scriptural provision, and since it so pointedly shows who it is that really is engaged in "depth counseling," and who on the other hand has but thin soup to offer, I am, nevertheless, quite willing to leave the matter right here and take up a different one.

What about a marriage that has been strained to its breaking point? Two people, let us say two *Christians,* fighting and arguing sit before a non-Christian counselor. As they spit out acrimonious words of bitterness and discouragement and declare that there is "nothing left" to their marriage, that they "loathe rather than love" one another, what does the unbelieving counselor have to offer? In this day of unparalleled marital failure, on what thin thread can he hang hope? From what source can he promise change? By what authority can he insist upon reconciliation (indeed, does he even believe reconciliation to be possible, or desirable)? Is he adequate?

---

[11]Cf. Jay Adams, *Shepherding God's Flock,* Vol. 1 (Presbyterian & Reformed Pub. Co.: Nutley, 1974), Appendix A, pp. 135-156 for a fuller discussion of grief as a counseling opportunity.

The scriptural counselor, in contrast, is able to meet the situation adequately. He says (in effect) with the full authority of God: "Since the information that you have given me indicates that you have no scriptural warrant for dissolving this marriage, there is but one course open to you: repentance and reconciliation followed by the building of an entirely new relationship that is pleasing to God." In contrast to the non-Christian, because he does not speak out of his own authority, the scriptural counselor speaks with confidence, knowing the goal and how to reach it. "Happily," he continues, "the Scriptures contain all of the information that you need to make these changes a reality, and—what is more—the Holy Spirit, who provided these instructions, promises also to give the strength to follow them, to all Christians who sincerely wish to do so and who step out in obedience by faith."

After detailing some of the many hopeful biblical specifics about such change (I shall not do so here as I have already done this elsewhere[12]), confidently he can encourage and persuade them: "If you mean business with God, even though your marriage presently is in a desperate condition, within a few weeks you can have instead a marriage that sings! Indeed, there is no reason why the first steps toward God's dramatic change cannot be taken *this week,* beginning *today.* What do you say?"

I ask you, *who* is adequate for such things? The answer: Christian counselors who use the Scriptures *authoritatively* to give *hope* through God's *promises* and *concrete instruction*—and no one else.

It is precisely because the will of God is made known authoritatively in these divinely inspired writings that the Christian may counsel with confidence. He does not need to guess about homosexuality or drunkenness, for

---

[12]Adams, *Competent to Counsel,* pp. 231ff.; *The Christian Counselor's Manual,* pp. 161-216.

instance, nor does he need to wait for the latest (changeable) scientific pronouncements to discover whether these human deviations stem from sickness or from learned behavior. God has spoken and clearly declared both to be *sins*. Therein lies hope. God has not promised to cure every illness, He has said nothing about changing genetic structures, but in Christ He has provided freedom from every *sin*. Together with a long string of similar difficulties, God has shown that those who trust Christ not only can be forgiven and cleansed, but also can fully overcome both of these sins. He says to converted Corinthians, using the past tense, "Such *were* some of you; but you were washed, but you were sanctified" (1 Cor. 6:11).

Absolute authority, Christ's commandments and precise pronouncements, are all but universally decried as restrictive and evil by those who eject the Scriptures from counseling. They make no distinction between authority and authoritarianism. Unwittingly thereby they jettison the basis for all hope, both for themselves and for their counselees.

When God authoritatively directs His children to forsake any sin or to follow any path of righteousness, the Christian may take hope. For apart from authoritative directions all is in flux, nothing is certain—there is no foundation for hope. Although his first reaction may be dismay when he recognizes how far his present life patterns have veered from God's way, upon repentance and further reflection the counselee should realize that whenever the heavenly Father requires anything of His children, He always provides instruction and power to meet those requirements. That means, for example, that when He says that we must "walk no longer as the Gentiles walk" (Ephesians 4:17) in Christ God will *enable* us to walk differently. Every directive of God—no matter how far short of it that we may come at the moment—serves to provide a solid foundation for the Christian's hope. Both counselor and counselee, therefore, may take heart in scriptural counseling for the very reason that it is authoritative.

"Still," you protest, "marriage counseling, like counseling the grief stricken, is not quite the same thing as dealing with those who are depressed, or those who exhibit bizarre behavior. What of the use of the Scriptures in those cases?"[13] Fair enough; let us consider another example. Fred's behavior, over a period of several years, at times became so bizarre that he was jailed, sent to two mental institutions, received a series of shock treatments, was placed on heavy medications and was subjected to intensive psychotherapy and various psychiatric treatments; all to no avail. When he came for scriptural counseling, it was as a last resort. But after six sessions his problem was solved. He has been leading a successful life as a productive Christian for over two years.

What made the difference? Biblical convictions. Since no evidence of organic damage or malfunction had been discovered during extensive medical tests, the Christian counselor rightly assumed that the roots of the problem were likely to be imbedded in the soil of sin. With that conviction he set to work.

His goal was not to treat symptoms (as had been done previously by those who administered shock treatments and by those who prescribed medication), nor was he intent upon discovering who had maltreated Fred in the past (as were others who had spent long hours dredging up all manner of parental and societal abuses in hopes of freeing the poor "victim" of a "tyrannical superego"). Nor

---

[13]Cf. Jay Adams, "A Christian View of Schizophrenia" in Peter Magaro (ed.), *The Construction of Madness* (Pergamon Press, Inc., Elmsford: 1975).

11

did the biblical counselor focus upon feelings (as a third group of counselors had when they spent months attempting, by reflecting his emotional responses, to draw solutions out of his own storehouse of resources). What did he do? Simply this: he set out in search of the sin or sins that he supposed were at the bottom of the difficulty. A few weeks later, through proper questioning, he discovered that Fred had been sinning against his body, the temple of the Holy Spirit, by failing to get adequate sleep. Every effect of LSD or other hallucinogenic drugs may be caused by significant sleep loss (an important fact for seminary students and faculty to remember during exam periods, incidentally). Fred's bizarre behavior always followed periods of sleep loss. Fred was convicted of his sin against God and, following forgiveness, was placed on a carefully monitored sleep regime, his daily schedule was revised according to biblical life priorities, and the problem was erased.

How did the counselor know to do this? Well, he went in search of sin because he believed the Bible. The Bible knows only two categories of causes for bizarre behavior: (1) organic causes, (2) non-organic causes. Organic factors may be hereditary or later acquired through accident, toxic destruction of brain cells, etc. Some—but not all—organic problems may be due to the sin of the individual (e.g., drug abuse may impair normal bodily functioning). On the other hand, all non-organic problems are represented in the Scriptures as stemming from the counselee's sin. There is no third, neutral category or subcategory that allows for non-organic difficulties for which the counselee may not be held personally responsible. On the basis of these biblical presuppositions, the Christian counselor began his search.

It is important to note that the Freudians and

Rogerians who treated Fred also did so *on the basis of their presuppositions.* The former presupposed that Fred's problem stemmed from past malsocialization; the latter, from failure to actualize his full potential. If Fred had been treated by a Skinnerian behaviorist, he too would have dealt with him on the basis of his conviction that man is only an animal and that a new set of environmental contingencies (or learning conditions) must be substituted for the previous ones which had brought about the undesirable behavior.

Every counselor, then, comes into counseling with presuppositions. These presuppositions pertain to all of the fundamental questions of life—its purpose (or lack of it), its problems, their solutions, the nature of man and the relationships which he sustains to others and to his world. Most important, every one of those presuppositions, wittingly or unwittingly, either includes or excludes God the Father, the Son, and the Holy Spirit. If, then, counseling begins with such presuppositions, how vital to begin with the right ones! And these are found only in the Scriptures.

Each counselor finds what he is searching for. The Freudian looks for others who "did it to him," and since parents, educators and even preachers and Sunday school teachers are sinners, he has little trouble finding many persons who have wronged the counselee. The Rogerian looks for insights from within the counselee that may be drawn out from a fully prepackaged supply of potential resources upon which the counselee has failed to rely. Since no sinful counselee lives up to his full potential, Rogerians may elicit some such insights. The Skinnerian looks for environmental changes that must be made in order to reshape his behavior. He will find much in the environment that needs to be altered. But, notice, not one of them looks for sin. Indeed, if he discovers it by accident, he renames it. Instead, the sin becomes an "emotional problem" or "immaturity" or "insecurity" or a "neurosis" or "mental illness" or something else that better fits the system built upon his unbiblical presuppositions.

Reinterpreting sin redirects one from real solutions involving regeneration, forgiveness, sanctification, etc., to some lesser inadequate remedy that never can satisfy the radical needs of condemned and corrupted man which took nothing less than the death of the Son of God to meet. Only scriptural counseling, grounded upon scriptural presuppositions, can do that.

Because of these facts, you must "be steadfast, immovable, always abounding in the work of the Lord, knowing that your labor is not in vain in the Lord" (I Cor. 15:58). When you counsel, it should be with hope, with expectation that since it is scriptural your efforts will not be in vain. If your counseling labors are done "in the Lord," that is, in obedience to His Word and in reliance upon His power, then they will issue in the Lord's results, in the Lord's time and in the Lord's way.

No other counselor has such assurance. At best, he knows that he has opted for some system (or eclectic amalgam from various systems) over against others. For a number of reasons this proves most dissatisfying. If he is a Freudian, he knows that more than half of the psychiatric world itself has abandoned his position and that vigorous attacks built upon strong arguments have been mounted against his views. Only the most arrogant psychiatrist today could be wholly "sold" on psychoanalysis if he has stood in full face of the prevailing winds. Moreover, look at the plethora of psychoanalytic cults, offshoots, and isms from which he must choose. Which sort of psychoanalysis will you have: classical Freudianism, neo-Freudianism, dynamic Freudianism, or what? Each of these differs from the next, not as conservative churches or denominations who agree on the fundamentals, but as widely as Orthodox Presbyterians and the Church of Rome. When one begins to branch out beyond the avowedly psychoanalytic schools to the existentialists, the Rogerians, the Behaviorists, the Transactional Analysts, the many sorts of group therapists, the Crisis Interventionists, the Rational Therapists, the Reality Therapists, the Radical Therapists, the Primal Screamers, the followers of Laing and so on and on and on, he begins to see that confusion reigns.

And unlike the Christian counselor, the rest have no standard, no way to know and no way to be sure who is right. What a difference it makes to have the authoritative Word of God!

The unbelieving counselor, seated in his plush, expensive furniture, surrounded by hundreds of books on psychology and psychiatry, with every word may seem to exude an outward confidence and certainty that one might have thought originated on Mount Olympus. Yet, unless he is incredibly naive, unless the volumes on his shelves are there for impression alone, he knows that every statement, that every judgment, that every decision that he makes in counseling is challenged and countered by scores of authors from an equal number of viewpoints. Psychiatric jargon or prestige, which may be heavily plastered over inner insecurities, ought never to be equated with psychiatric knowledge or wisdom.[14]

The truth of the matter is that the Christian counselor who determines by the grace of God to know and use the Scriptures in his counseling is the only one who can ever have a solid basis for what he says and does. While there may be any number of issues about which he has not yet

---

[14]For interesting comments on this subject, see David S. Viscott, *The Making of a Psychiatrist* (Greenwich, 1972), pp. 24,25,84.

15

come to a fully biblical understanding, nevertheless, because he has the Scriptures, on all of the fundamental questions of life he not only knows but is fully assured of the truth and of the will of God.

Let no one, therefore, tell you that the scriptural counselor is inadequate and that he must take a back seat while learning from his pagan counterpart. The opposite is true, and it is about time that Christian counselors began to make the fact known.

In closing, I cannot help but think of the Psalmist when he wrote: "I have more insight than all my teachers, for your testimonies are my meditation" (Ps. 119:99). To those of you who believe this, let your prayer, together with him, be:

> Sustain me according to your Word that I may live; and do not let me be put to shame because of my hope (Ps. 119:116).

CHAPTER II
Understanding Problems Biblically

The use of the Scriptures in counseling involves the interaction of no less than five essential factors. These are:

1. a biblical understanding of the counselee's problem, stemming from. . .

2. a clear understanding of the Holy Spirit's *telos* in scriptural passages appropriate to both the problem and the solution, and. . .

3. a meeting of man's problem and God's full solution in counseling, according to. . .

4. the formulation of a biblical plan of action, leading toward. . .

5. commitment to scriptural action by the counselee. . .

all prayerfully accomplished by the enabling power (grace) of the Holy Spirit. It will be necessary to examine each of these five factors in some detail.

The Counselor Must Reach a Biblical Understanding of the Counselee's Problem

As you can see from that statement, biblical counselors cannot be satisfied simply to trust the word of the counselee, the report of some referring agency, the conclusions of standardized tests, or even their own first impressions about the counselee's problem. Rather, they must engage in a twofold process of research: (1) They

17

must search out, discover and interpret according to biblical norms all of the significant data concerning the problem that may be provided by the counselee, parents, spouse, or others who may be involved. Data, we have shown elsewhere, are not limited to verbal material obtained during counseling sessions.[1] Written information, in the form of lists prepared by counselees, records kept on Discovering Problem Pattern forms, failures and difficulties encountered in accomplishing initial homework assignments, as well as many sorts of non-verbal or halo behavior, are examples of other important sources for obtaining data.

Today's mail brings a letter from a Christian physician overseas who is working in tandem with a graduate of our counseling program whom we shall call John. He writes:

> The problem of generalizing was mine last week with a bank manager patient whom I could not persuade to go back to work. . . . I thought it was that he had made the bank his idol, and the image was beginning to crack. . . however John got through to the problem straight away when he found that in fact the man had been storing up resentment over a senior man's laziness to such a degree (while blandly going on maintaining a stiff upper lip English smile) that he could not face going into the bank anymore.

Notice several facts in that account. First, note how he says, "John got through to the problem. . . when he *found* . . . ." While I do not know the details of the case, from the brief record at least three things seem to be apparent: (a) John probed for the significant data. Prior to counseling, the bank manager had been disguising the true problem which John had to "find"; (b) the physician, even though (rightly) thinking in biblical categories ("I thought that he had made the bank his idol. . ."), was wrong in his original

---

[1]Jay E. Adams, *The Christian Counselor's Manual,* pp. 257-59, 308, 310, 313-16.

assumption because he did not gather the significant data necessary to make a correct evaluation of the problem (probably he did not have adequate time to do so and, therefore, referred the counselee to John); (c) these data, when discovered, were analyzed and defined biblically. Judged by scriptural norms, John and his colleague rightly discussed the problem in biblical terms. They concluded: "the man had been storing up resentment." One can see that, behind that evaluation, these biblical counselors were vitally aware of such passages as Ephesians 4:26b: "Do not let the sun go down on your anger." They did not label the problem as a neurosis or blunt the truth by excusing the counselee's behavior as a justifiable "defense mechanism." Nor in this case did they speak even of "repression" (a word that carries heavy Freudian freight). They labelled the sin biblically for what it was—resentment.

Other labels at first might be considered kindlier; but in fact they are not. John and his friend are doing the kindest thing possible in calling sin "sin." There is no hope in speaking of neuroses, defense mechanisms or repressions; God has not promised to do anything about such problems. But every Christian knows that Jesus came to deal with sin. Labeling sin "sin" then is kindly because it gives hope; it points to the true problem and to God's solution.

Other labels not only remove hope and confuse the situation, but point in wrong directions. Psychiatric labels point toward psychiatric solutions. Thus they redirect both counselor and counselee away from the Scriptures. No one recommends repentance as the solution for neurosis! When the true problem, therefore, is sin, all such misdirection is cruel because it points away from the only true solution to the counselee's problem and, of even greater moment, is the fact that this redirection itself is sin. Ultimately it constitutes rebellion against God by the rejection of His Word, His Son and His Spirit as irrelevant or inadequate.[2]

It is important, then, for Christian counselors to discover all of the relevant data concerning the counselee's problem(s) and to interpret the meaning of these data biblically. If there is an organic base, or if there are organic aspects to the problem, he will want to know this so that he may be able to enlist medical help in accordance with biblical principles.[3] If the difficulty is a non-organic problem in living, he will want to call sin "sin" and handle it accordingly. Nothing is of more importance to the entire counseling process than the foundation; if that is out of line, all else is likely to be off kilter too.

(2) The other side of the research process in which the counselor must engage before, during, and after every counseling session involves the discovery of the biblical norms by which symptoms, behavior, and other data may

---

[2]This is a very common failing among Christians who are psychiatrists or psychologists. Take, for example, the words of David A. Blaiklock in his book *Release From Tension* (Grand Rapids, 1969), in which he advocates altering the biblical picture for the benefit of the counselee: "Thus it behooves Christians who have little tendency to worry to make a worrying Christian's lot harder by loading him with guilt produced by their condemnation of the 'sin of worry,' without leading him gently to the true answer" (p. 49). Blaiklock thinks that he has a truer answer than the biblical answer which is that worry is a violation of God's commandment (Matt. 6:31,34; Phil. 4:6) and therefore is sin. Blaiklock thinks not. What does he think is truer about worry? He says that it is in part hereditary (p. 49), but of more importance is—"the effect of the vital first five years" (p. 50). That is truer, kinder? Sin, as every believer knows, can be removed in Christ. But what hope is there for the "hereditary" worrier who is also stuck with past programming? Blaiklock, because he thinks he can be kinder than the Scriptures, cruelly takes away the worrying believer's hope. Fortunately it can be restored, for in every directive of God to His children there is hope; directives speak of possibility. He never directs them without providing the means for fulfilling His directives. Cf. Jay Adams, *What To Do About Worry* (Nutley, 1971).

[3]Cf. Jay E. Adams, pp. 105ff., and *The Christian Counselor's Manual*, pp. 437-43.

20

be evaluated and understood. In order to label problems biblically, he will need to know, for instance, that the Scriptures describe drunkenness as sin. He will not approach the problem under any illusion that the counselee is suffering from "the disease of alcoholism" (whatever that may be).

Because such research requires the kind of knowledge of the Scriptures that Paul describes as "the word of Christ dwelling richly within" (Col. 3:16),[4] the best background for a Christian counselor is not training in psychology or psychiatry, but a good theological seminary education. He will need to know how to exegete the Scriptures, faithfully studying them regularly in order to steep himself in God's promises, warnings, prohibitions, injunctions, and methods. The good counselor will be helpful because he brings a "rich" supply of biblical truth into the counseling situation. From this supply he can retrieve much material previously studied, understood, and stored up for just such occasions.

Not every sort of exegesis, however, can so supply the counselor; Paul is speaking of exegesis with a practical slant (it is Christ's word ministered to others "with all wisdom" that he has in mind). But how does one acquire this sort of exegetical capability? The only adequate way for a counselor to learn to exegete the Scriptures in a practical (rather than in a merely theoretical) manner is to begin to exegete the Scriptures *personally.* That is to say, mere storage of facts is not in view in Paul's words "richly dwelling within," but rather facts transformed into life. Good counselors are concerned about becoming wise in their own personal living and, as a result, they also become wise in the ministry of the Word to others.

------

[4]For further discussion of counselor qualifications, cf. Adams, *Competent to Counsel,* pp. 59ff., and *The Christian Counselor's Manual,* pp. 13-15.

In the sort of study contemplated, then, the counselor does not study *first* for information to use in preaching or in counseling. Instead, he studies always with an eye on his own life. As he does so, the understanding of a verb form may bring conviction of sin, the import of a personal pronoun may occasion a burst of song or thanksgiving. Such study is not abstract; it requires personally involved exegesis. In this study the counselor's own life in relationship to God and his neighbor is always under review. He studies *beneath* rather than *above* the Scriptures. And. . . it is just *because* he has experienced the truth of God exposing his own sin, piercing through every joint to the marrow, judging the desires and thoughts of his heart, encouraging by its promises, comforting, healing, motivating—that he is able to minister that same Word to others in wisdom.

Since the counselee's non-organic problems are hamartiagenic ("sin-engendered"), the counselor himself is familiar with them. They are not different in kind from his own. Therefore, the solutions that he has found *personally* he is able to use *practically*. By this I do not mean that he must experience every situation in exactly the same way that the counselee has. He does not need to sin every sin; to commit adultery in order to know how to help an adulterer. The temptations spun out of his own adulterous heart, as well as the possibility of generalizing from biblical help that he has received in other sin experiences, are quite adequate to enable him to minister the Word sympathetically. With Paul, he is able to "comfort those who are afflicted" with the "same comfort" that he received "when afflicted" (although afflicted, perhaps, in quite a different way). This, Paul says, he can do for those who are "in *any* affliction" (cf. 2 Cor. 1:3-7).

So we see first of all that in his use of the Scriptures in

counseling the Christian counselor must depend upon the Bible from the outset to obtain a biblical understanding of the counselee's problem(s). This understanding may be reached only by researching the problem according to biblical methods, out of biblical motives, using biblical categories for definition and labeling. And it can never be purely academic, for counseling from start to finish deals with matters in which every counselor himself is intimately involved.

We must turn now to the second factor that is always present whenever the Scriptures are used properly in counseling.

CHAPTER III
Understanding the Scriptures Telically

A Clear Understanding of the Holy Spirit's *Telos* in Scriptural Passages Appropriate to Both the Problem and the Solution

Note well, the *telos* (or purpose) of a passage should be central to everything that is done in counseling; that means that it is the vital factor even in the selection of the passage *as appropriate* to the problem at hand.

The *telic* side of exegesis has been either ignored, underplayed, or unknown by many pastors. Sadly this fact is all too apparent to those who have studied this question in the history of preaching. If any one fact is evident, it is this: preachers, good Christian men who meant well, nevertheless have persisted in using the Scriptures for their own purposes rather than for the purposes for which they were given. Often because blissfully unaware of the Holy Spirit's intention in placing a passage where it occurs, they have generated the most incredible interpretations and dogmas and have given some of the most horrendous advice, all in the name of God. Fortunately, on the other hand, in God's providence much truth has been preached from passages that say nothing about it! And all that may be said about the vital place that *telic* exegesis must play in preaching pertains with equal force to the use of the Scriptures in Christian counseling.

I have spoken already about the importance of authority in counseling.[1] Authority arises from knowing

---

[1]But see also Jay Adams, *Shepherding God's Flock,* Vol. II, pp. 14,105ff.

that what the counselor says truly comes from God. That cannot be known unless the counselor shows the counselee that the directive, warning, or promise about which he is speaking comes from the Scriptures. The authority will be lacking unless (a) the counselor knows the *telos* of the passage, (b) uses it for the same purpose as that for which the Holy Spirit gave it, and (c) demonstrates to the counselee that this is in truth its purpose and meaning. Because the matter under discussion is of such vital importance, I shall linger for a while over each of those necessary elements in establishing scriptural authority for one's counsel. With Paul, the counselor must be able to say in good conscience, "For I do not, like so many, peddle an adulterated message of God" (II Cor. 2:17).

(a) The counselor must know the *telos* of every passage that he uses in counseling. It is not enough to understand the grammatical-historical, biblical-theological or systematic, and rhetorical aspects of a passage. These are essential, and I should be the last one to say anything to undermine such work, for each of these elements plays a vital part in biblical exegesis. Indeed, without their assistance often it is impossible either to discover the *telos* or to be sure even when one has done so. Yet it is possible to have all of these matters in mind in exegesis and still *misuse* a portion of Scripture in preaching or counseling. Thus, the story of the Seeking Father and the Pouting Elder Brother instead becomes the Parable of the Prodigal Son; the two commandments to love God and neighbor are psychologized by those who want to add to them a third commandment, "love yourself," which they then make basic to the other two, in spite of the fact that this is a thought repugnant to the entire Bible, and the clear statement of Christ that he is speaking of *two* commandments only: "On these *two* commandments hang all the law and the prophets."

25

(b) The counselor must know the *purpose* of the passage; that is, he must know what God intended to do to the reader (warn, encourage, motivate, ec.) with those words. Then, he must make God's purpose his own in the application of the passage to human needs. But to do this he must develop an exegetical conscience by which he determines never to use a passage for any purpose other than that purpose, or those purposes for which God gave it (often, of course, there are sub *tele* involved in a larger telic unit). This determination will make him faithful not only as an interpreter, but also in his *use* of the Scriptures.

It was at this point that some Puritan preachers and commentators set Protestantism back several generations. They abandoned the superior method used by Calvin which focused upon telic matters in the text. Instead, it became their practice to discuss lengthy questions from the whole corpus of systematic theology as these had any bearing upon a word or phrase, no matter how remote that connection might be. Contextually there was no warrant for this practice; and, indeed, it often obscured important contextual connections and distracted one from the main purpose and proper use of the passage. No wonder many of their commentaries were interminable. And to these doctrinal discussions some of them often appended a series of "improvements" or "uses" of the text. Under such rubrics every sort of tenuous and sometimes moralizing relationship of the passage to life was explored. The passage was wrung dry.

God's words must be used to achieve God's purposes. Obviously, therefore, flip-and-point methods of using the Scriptures are taboo, since they ignore telic considerations. Along with such techniques we must reject Bible prescription methods in which the counselor in effect tears out a page of Scripture and hands it to the counselee without explanation as the remedy for his problem.[2] For all of the understanding of it that he has, it might have been scrawled in a Latin that can be translated only by a pharmacist! All of which leads to the third point.

(c) The Scriptures must be "opened" (i.e., "explained," cf. Luke 24:32) if counselors would have the hearts of their counselees to burn within them like those of the disciples who walked the Emmaus road with Christ. When *He* is disclosed to them as the subject of "all" of the Scriptures, moralizing will disappear, irrelevant material will evaporate and the *telos* of the passage will find its proper place in Christ.

But how does one discover the *telos* of any passage? (1) By studying with the *telic* goal in mind (one rarely finds what he does not seek), and in that search (2) by looking for *telic* cues. Often these cues are overt; but some are more evident than others. Some *telic* statements have to do with the *whole* of the Scriptures, as for example when Paul wrote that the Scriptures have two purposes: "to make one wise unto salvation" and to "teach, convict, correct, and train in righteousness" (II Tim. 3:15-16). Thus any given passage primarily will have either an evangelis-

---

[2] Not that God in His wise providence cannot use His Word even when given in this form. Ordinarily what is meant by handing out Scripture verses like prescriptions is that the Bible is used in a magical manner, much more like a talisman than a divine Revelation. The Bible passage (like a prescription) is supposed to effect results whether understood by the recipient or not. All such usage is itself unbiblical and must be rejected. But Jim, a physician friend of mine, objects to the rejection of the image of the prescription. "Instead of stressing the aspects just mentioned," he observes, "why not focus upon the positive (highly instructive) aspects of the comparison, like the need for careful diagnosis, the need for a thorough knowledge of medicines and their effects, etc., all of which have to do with *care* by the doctor, or in your case by the counselor?" He has a point! If we take Jim's word to heart, we shall note the essential differences between counseling and the writing of medical prescriptions, and end up with *both* the ideas of care on the part of the counselor and understanding and commitment by the counselee.

tic or edificational goal. In Luke 24:27, Christ referred to Himself as the subject of "all of the Scriptures," which is perhaps the most basic and comprehensive *telos* of all. Christ Himself is the Savior and Head of His church who has made salvation and Christian growth a reality. The Christian counselor, therefore, must see Christ in every passage that he uses and introduce the counselee to Him there. This means that he may never use the Scriptures moralistically or humanistically. But, while never forgetting this redemptive base, he also must select passages because of their particular *telic* emphases, beginning broadly by dividing Bible books and counseling portions, according to their major emphases, into the two main purposes mentioned above: evangelism and edification.

John's gospel and first epistle provide the most obvious sorts of *telic* notes: the first was "written. . . that you may *believe,*" and the second "written to you who believe. . . that you may *know.*" Is there any wonder then that verses like John 1:12; 3:16; 3:36; 5:24; 14:1-6 and many others have been used so frequently by the Spirit of God to bring men to belief? After all, the Gospel of John, we are clearly told, was written for this very purpose. Likewise one should turn to the first epistle when counseling with a believer who lacks assurance of salvation. This is particularly necessary when counseling those who today similarly are plagued with a new kind of legalistic Gnosticism that teaches that only a small group of persons has a right to assurance. Characteristically, such preachers use I John not to bring assurance but to destroy what they believe to be false assurance. God's purpose in the book is positive, theirs negative.[3]

Portions of biblical books are devoted to different

---

[3]A frequently observed problem of preachers is that of using a passage that has a positive *telos* negatively.

purposes. When the writer of Hebrews says, "Therefore leaving the elementary teaching about Christ, let us press on. . ." (6:1), he is giving the reader a *telic* cue to a shift in emphasis (all, of course, within the scope of the broader *telos* or tele for which the book of Hebrews was written). Ephesians 1-3 cannot be separated from Ephesians 4-6, since the two sections are hinged together by that crucial "therefore" in Ephesians 4:1 which shows that the doctrine taught in the first half has vital implications for the practical Christian living enjoined in the second half. Yet, it is important for the counselor to know that the latter portion of Ephesians shows *how* Christians, as members of Christ's redeemed body (the theme of the former), can learn to function together in love and unity.

Phrases like "Brethren, I would not have you to be ignorant concerning. . ." (I Thess. 4:13); "Wherefore, comfort one another with these words" (I Thess. 4:18); "I have written. . . to encourage you and to testify that this is the true grace of God" (I Peter 5:12); "I wish, therefore, always to remind you of these matters. . ." (II Peter 1:12,13); "I am writing you to arouse your pure minds by way of remembrance" (II Peter 3:1); "I found it necessary to write you appealing that you vigorously defend the faith once for all delivered to the saints" (Jude 3); "prescribe and teach these things" (I Tim. 4:11); "remind them of these things and solemnly charge them in the presence of God. . ." (II Tim. 2:14) are just a few of the many *telic* cues by which the counselor can be guided infallibly in determining the Holy Spirit's intentions in any given passage of the Scriptures.

Even when *telic* cues do not appear overtly, the *telic* quest still must be carried on. And this quest may be pursued successfully, for although the *tele* may not always be as apparent as in the New Testament examples mentioned above, they may be found by looking for *telic* thrusts and emphases. Thus, for example, there are few overt *telic* cues in Philippians, but the student who seeks to discover the main *tele* behind the writing of that book will have little trouble uncovering such purposes as (a) Paul's desire to thank the Philippians for their gift, (b) his concern to explain the working of God's providence in his imprisonment, (c) his interest in healing the division in the Philippian church, and (d) his wish to calm their fears about Epaphroditus.

"The *telic* note is important, I can see, for establishing authority in counseling and thus assuring both the counselor and counselee that the analysis of his problem and the solutions offered are well founded, but how does this work in actual practice?" you may ask. This important question leads naturally into a discussion of the third factor.

CHAPTER IV

Bringing These Two Understandings Together

There Must Be a Meeting of Man's Problem and God's Full Solution in Counseling

Let us begin by comparing the approaches of two counselors at work. They both face the same problem: young parents have come seeking help in the discipline of seven-year-old Johnny, their first and only child. Johnny, like all other seven year olds, is a sinner who, in this case, has been allowed to develop a disturbingly rebellious sinful life style through parental permissiveness occasioned by their fear, poor instruction, and general laziness.

One minister, steeped in the modified Rogerianistic-behaviorism advocated in some recent books by Christian authors who have baptized such strange views into the faith unconverted,[1] finds himself in difficult straits since he considers spanking a "last resort." He points to Proverbs 23:7 and reads "As a man thinketh in his heart, so is he." From that proof text he develops the thesis for the parents that they must carefully instruct their child about the reasons for the family rules so that through proper understanding of these, at length correct behavior may be achieved. It does not take a prophet to predict the consequences of such an approach.

In contrast, a thoroughly biblical counselor will handle

---

[1]Cf., e.g., Bruce Narramore, *Help I'm A Parent* (Grand Rapids, 1972), in which spanking is considered "a last resort" to be used only "when all other methods have failed" (pp. 107-8).

the problem quite differently. To begin with, he will think of the *problem* biblically—that is, rebellious behavior is *sin.* Because he sees the problem in those terms rather than as a problem in understanding, he will move toward a different sort of solution. Having rejected the compromise with behaviorism that leads to the notion that spanking is a last resort, instead he will urge these parents to use it consistently as a vital biblical disciplinary method. He will turn for instruction to Proverbs 22:15, "Foolishness is bound up in the heart of a child, but the rod of discipline will drive it far from him."[2] But he also will instruct them that punishment is not enough; together with the punishment the child must be confronted nouthetically about his sin and his need for a Savior who can change him, and whose redemptive help he needs to overcome his sin. In order to emphasize this balanced two-pronged scriptural approach, he will discuss Proverbs 29:15, "The rod *and* reproof give wisdom, but an undisciplined child causes his mother shame," and Ephesians 6:4: "Fathers. . . bring up your children in the discipline *and* nouthetic confrontation of the Lord."[3]

Because of his eclectic approach, the first counselor has been influenced to use the Scriptures superficially. He comes to the Scriptures prejudiced by his psychological rather than biblical background. Careful grammatical-historical, contextual, systematic and *telic* use of the

---

[2]He might calm any fears that they may have over using spanking in punishment by discussing Prov. 23:13-14, a passage intended to give reassurance and from which he also will want to explain that such obedience as the rod brings is essential to creating conditions in which to teach children the way of salvation (v. 14).

[3]He will not fail to stress biblical rewards either, noting (as Paul observes in Eph. 6:1 when quoting the children's commandment) that the commandment to "honor" one's "father and mother" is "the first commandment with a *promise"* (reward).

Scriptures by the second pastor leads him to avoid such errors. He moves in the right direction because his basic commitment is to the Bible rather than to psychological or psychiatric theory. First, because he is biblically based, he rejects Rogerian and Behavioristic inroads. Secondly, because he is careful about his exegesis, he cannot settle for a superficial use of Proverbs 23:7: "As a man thinketh in his heart, so is he." Unlike many of the proverbs, that verse has a context. It is part of a warning against taking the words of one's host seriously when he urges you to eat more food. The exegete does not wrench it from that setting. Rather, properly translating and using the verse *for the purpose for which it was given,* he understands it to say, as the Berkeley version more accurately translates it:

> Eat not the bread of him whose eye is selfish, neither desire his delicacies, *for as one who inwardly figures the cost so is he;* "eat and drink," he says to you, but his heart is not with you.

He does not fall into the trap of developing a false philosophical, psychological, or counseling principle that says, "changed behavior flows only from changed understanding" from this verse. Rather, as he reflects upon the biblical passages that *do* speak of changing behavior through discipline, he discovers that *both* the rod and reproof (which further investigation shows involves what the New Testament calls nouthetic admonition) "give wisdom" (Prov. 29:15). His psychological theory, then, develops *from* the scriptural data; it is not superimposed upon the Scriptures. Because it does, it will not cramp him but rather will allow room enough for different sorts of changes to be effected through different sorts of discipline.

Because the former counselor's thinking is not fully biblical from start to finish, his view of discipline is narrowed and restricted. The latter, willing to submit to the Word of God, is free to reject all other theories that contradict and to open himself fully to the breadth of biblical truth. The former cannot see how a change in living also can lead to a change of thinking. He cannot understand how the rod can drive out foolishness and give wisdom, for he is chained to the psychological notions (weakly supported by a biblical passage that has nothing to do with the subject) that rules always must be explained in order to be effective and that changes in behavior always must be preceded by changes in thought. The real problem, you see, arises when one interprets the Scriptures in the light of modern thought, according to his own superficial exegesis or in some other way that allows the Scriptures only to trickle through a man-made funnel. The full message of the Bible, thus, is withheld and scriptural authority is weakened.

Let us consider another example. In his book, *The Bible in Pastoral Care,* Wayne Oates suggests using the Bible as a kind of Rorschach test or (as he actually calls the recommended practice) the pastor's "thematic apperception test." Quoting the liberal, Oskar Pfister[4] with approval when he wrote, "Tell me what you find in the Bible, and I will tell you what you are," Oates says that the Bible must be seen as "a means of insight into the deeper problems of people."[5] By this he does not mean that the Bible's *content* reveals these insights, but that the *use* that one makes of the Bible will give the counselor insight. Bad as that may be, I quote it not to show how far astray that counselors may go in using the Bible in ways in which it was never intended to be used, but rather as background for the particular misuse of the Scriptures

---

[4]Pfister was a psychoanalyst and good friend of Freud as well as a liberal pastor.

[5]Wayne E. Oates, *The Bible in Pastoral Care* (Philadelphia, 1953), pp. 22-23.

that Oates demonstrates when trying to support his "apperception" thesis, namely, the practice of *projecting one's own ideas into the text*. The apperception idea is an indorsement of the practice of projection, and Oates' misuse of the Scriptures in attempting to find biblical support itself quite adequately illustrates and demonstrates the practice! He turns to James 1:22-24.

> Be doers of the word, and not hearers only, deceiving yourselves. For if any one is a hearer of the word and not a doer, he is like a man who observes his natural face in a mirror; for he observes himself and goes away and at once forgets what he was like.

Then he comments:

> The implication is that the Bible is a mirror into which a person projects his own concept of himself, and which in turn reflects it back with accuracy.[6]

I shall not take your time to comment on this "projective exegesis" by which Oates attempts to find scriptural support for the unbiblical and exceedingly dangerous practice of a projective use of the Bible. If the quotation itself is not sufficient warning against the practice, any argumentation would be unconvincing. Clearly Oates has a theory to support; so he comes to the Bible and grinds his axe upon it. *Telic* considerations, contextual exegesis and biblical theological understandings all give way to a projective psychologizing of the text.

One of the most commonly found examples of the projection of psychological concepts external to the Scriptures into the Bible is the practice (to which I alluded earlier) of "discovering" in the Bible that Christ really summed up the whole law in three rather than two commandments. The sober fact is that He did not. When Christ spoke of two commandments: love for God and

---

[6]*Ibid.*

love for one's neighbor (Matt. 22:34-40), He intended to say exactly that and nothing else. Yet psychologizing Christians have added a third even more basic commandment: love yourself. Some go so far as to claim that unless a person first learns to love himself properly, he will never learn to love his neighbor.

The argument sounds somewhat plausible at first, for how can one know how to love another unless he knows how to love himself? If he thinks (wrongly) that a practice is desirable, he may urge it upon his neighbor to his injury. And, after all, isn't that what Jesus meant by the words "as yourself"?

But a moment's reflection shows that all such argumentation misses the point—the Scriptures, not one's personal experience, must tell us what constitutes love to another. One cannot go wrong in loving another when he does what the Bible says.

When Christ urged Christians to love their neighbors as themselves, He did not intend to say that this would entail doing for another precisely what one does for himself. Instead (as in Christ's "first" commandment) the stress in the "second" is upon the intensity and devotedness of the love rather than upon the identity or similarity of action. Remember, Jesus pointed out that the second is *like* the first. The words, "as yourself" in the second parallel the phrase in the first commandment to love God "with all your heart. . . ." The emphasis is not upon the content of the love (that is found in the commandments themselves), but upon its fervency and genuineness: "Love God as *enthusiastically* as you love yourself." Beyond this, the fact that Christ distinguishes only "two commandments" (v. 40) itself is decisive.

Psychologizing the passage leads to pernicious errors. (1) God's Word is misrepresented. (2) One's own life rather than God's Word becomes the standard for behavior. (3) Endless speculation over matters like proper and improper "self love" and "self concept" is generated. It is very dangerous to make a big point over that about which Christ made no point at all (indeed, He explicitly excluded it by the word "two").

Elsewhere I have considered this matter more fully.[7] Here, let me simply say one more word. Counselors who focus on improving self-concepts and who try to teach counselees how to love themselves will find themselves spinning their wheels. Much time and energy can be wasted trying to strengthen egos. Not one word in the Scriptures encourages such activities. They are as futile as the pursuit of happiness. For a good self-concept never arises from seeking it directly. It is the by-product of loving God and one's neighbor. The Christian who concentrates on those two commandments will have little problem with the "third," for Jesus said, "He who has found his life shall lose it, and he who has lost his life for my sake shall find it" (Matt. 10:39).

Let me summarize what I have said. First, the counselee's problem must be understood and evaluated scripturally. Secondly, the Holy Spirit's *telos* in every passage used in counseling must be sought and, when found, must govern its use; and thirdly, there must be a meeting of man's problem and God's full solution. These goals can be achieved only by counselors who allow neither a distortion, dilution, nor admixture of the biblical data to enter the counseling situation, whether introduced by the counselee or by their own misuse of the Scriptures. Nothing less than this is the biblical norm against which we must measure our counseling and toward which we must ask God's Spirit to enable us to make progress continually.

---

[7]Adams, *The Christian Counselor's Manual*, pp. 142-44.

CHAPTER V
Forming Biblical Plans of Action

"I'm OK; You're OK"—the words may be modern, but the idea behind them is not new. They represent exactly the false, humanistic viewpoint of the rich young ruler when he called Christ "Good Master." When Tom Harris urges us to become OK by means of Transactional Analysis, he is asking us to do so without the aid of the Christ of the Scriptures. After all, he tells us, "truth is not. . . bound in a black book."[1]

Because the rich young ruler thought he was OK and that Christ was OK (in the same way), Jesus challenged his use of the word: "Why do you call me good? There is no one who is good except God" (Luke 18:19). Whenever it appears, that concept of goodness must be challenged. First, the rich young ruler could not be allowed to continue to think of Christ as good in the same sense in which he considered himself good. Unless he was willing to admit that Jesus was God, he would have to revise his language to fit the facts. All others are sinners. On the other hand, he needed to see just that—*he* was a sinner. Outwardly he had conformed to the Law, but inwardly he had broken it all as Christ so clearly demonstrated by exposing his idolatrous worship of riches.

Transactional Analysis and all other unscriptural systems that seek to change men likewise fail on both of these counts: (1) they underestimate man's problem, and

---

[1]Thomas A. Harris, *I'm OK—You're OK* (New York, 1967), p. 230.

consequently (2) they underestimate what it takes to solve that problem. Freudians view the counselee as a victim of poor socialization and, therefore, think that since the problem was brought about by man, man can solve it. The expert analyst/therapist can undo (at least) some of what man has done. The Rogerians think man is good at the core and his problem is a failure to actualize untapped resources. Hence, they attempt to draw out from him the answers that they believe he has the capability of producing. The solution lies in realizing his potential. He, rather than others, is his problem, but by the same token, he is also his own adequate solution. Behaviorists, who think that all human problems stem from poor learning caused by faulty conditioning, naturally see the solution in relearning through reconditioning. The manipulation of environmental contingencies is what is needed. Transactional Analysis sees crossed transactions (or relationships) as the problem. This situation may be remedied by learning to make paired transactions on the adult level. In all of these systems, and indeed in every non-biblical counseling system, man is the measure of all things.

But into the midst of this humanistic confusion God interposes His divine revelation—the Bible. From this Book we learn that we are all *not* OK. Indeed, our condition is not repairable. Our problem is sin. We have rebelled against our holy Creator, breaking His laws and incurring His wrath. As sinners, we cannot manufacture holiness with dirty hands. A righteous God has declared that He will punish us for our sin. We have no way in ourselves, through other sinful human beings, or by the manipulation of the environment, of appeasing Him. If, like Job, we try to speak to Him on the same transactional level, He Himself crosses out our transaction as He declares, "Who is this that darkens counsel by words without knowledge?" (Job 38:2).[2] But when, instead, we recognize our sin, become "as a child," and trust in complete dependence upon the sinless Son of God, who died for our sins and rose bodily from the dead, we receive forgiveness and learn the joy of the Cross transaction by which we say "Abba" to our loving heavenly Father. Our problem is not an immaturity that can be solved by becoming more adult; like the rich young ruler, we think we have come of age when our greatest need is to become like a little child.

We have discussed three of the five factors in scriptural counseling. Let us now consider the fourth factor in scriptural counseling.

The Counselor Must Help the Counselee to Formulate a Biblical Plan of Action

You can see that this is exactly what is missing in each of the schemes just mentioned. The adherents to these schemes do not depend upon the Bible for help. Nor can they. Their systems do not allow for God's Word. Freudians think that the Bible is part of the problem rather than the source of solutions. Rogerians see no need for any outside help; to them the Bible is irrelevant. Behaviorists consider Scripture but myth that must be removed as a harmful or (at best) useless contingency, and the Transactional Analysis people find in the Bible a major reason for the crossed parent/child transactional problems that they wish to combat.

Scriptural counseling does not mix well with other ingredients. Those who propound other theories know this and often say so (Freud, for instance, called religion a neurosis.); when will Christians become aware of the

---

[2]T. A. fundamentally constitutes an attack upon all authority structures, which means that it is (at bottom) an attack upon God Himself who is the Ultimate authority.

incompatibility and likewise say so? It is time for us to stand up and echo God's declaration: "My thoughts are not your thoughts. Neither are your ways my ways" (Isa. 55:8). Apart from the Scriptures, no man's plans can be adequate. When God commands, "Let the wicked forsake his way, and the unrighteous man his thoughts; and let him return to the Lord" (Isa. 55:7), He is speaking of the *only* road to forgiveness. He continues, "let him return to the Lord. . . For He will abundantly pardon" (Isa. 55:7). It is clear that Isaiah was foreshadowing the words of Jesus when He said, "I am *the* way. . . no one comes to the Father but by me" (John 14:6). How could it be otherwise? How could we think that humanistic analyses of man's problems could lead to Christian theistic solutions? When will we come to see that there are not twenty ways or four ways, but only two—God's way and all others?

Listen to Isaiah again: "For as the heavens are higher than the earth, so are my ways higher than your ways, and my thoughts than your thoughts" (Isa. 55:9). And once more, Isaiah connects the ability to return to God with a power that comes from His own Word. That word, like the rain and snow that do not return to heaven before they water the earth and bring forth fruit, will not return void. It too will bear fruit, accomplishing the purpose for which it is sent. Remember that this fifty-fifth chapter of Isaiah opens with an invitation to all those who are in need: "Ho everyone who thirsts, come. . . ." You might have supposed that the prophet was speaking to psychoanalytic patients who had been paying fifty dollars for a half hour's treatment when he asks: How much longer will God's people "spend money for what is not bread, and wages for what does not satisfy?" (Isa. 55:1,2). All psychological and psychiatric systems that reject the Bible must themselves be rejected for that very reason. Since the

41

message of God's Word is what is needed, therefore, and since no one else will turn to the Scriptures to find it, it is incumbent upon the Christian counselor to help the counselee to formulate a biblical plan of action.

What is a biblical plan of action and how may it be formulated? A biblical plan of action (1) grows out of and at every point is consistent with biblical presuppositions and principles, (2) aims at biblical goals, (3) depends upon biblical methods, and (4) is pursued and accomplished from biblical motives. It is a plan in which the yeasty principles and practices of the Scriptures have been kneaded into the dough of the situation so that they permeate all.

(1) When I say that a biblical plan of action grows out of and at every point is consistent with biblical presuppositions and principles, I hope to distinguish between two things: those biblical directives, warnings, promises, and so forth, that apply specifically to the counselee's problem, and those that apply in a more general way. While the Scriptures deal with *every* situation that the Christian minister faces in the course of his legitimate work, while they contain all of the data that are necessary for life and godliness, this information comes neither in the form of an encyclopedia, nor as a ready reference manual. Rather, God, in His wisdom, gave it to us in many different forms—narrative, poetry, letters, songs, prophecies, apocalyptic, drama, gospel, wisdom literature, and proverbs—from which the presuppositions and principles must be derived. Not infrequently, of course, these principles are stated directly and at times even propositionally.

Often, the very situation faced by the counselor was handled in the biblical record. This is to be expected since sinners and their problems have not changed all that much. Thus, when Paul wrote, "Fathers do not provoke your children to anger but bring them up in the discipline and nouthetic confrontation of the Lord" (Eph. 6:4), he was giving directions that can be applied explicitly to every Christian parent in every era. The way that God disciplines is the norm by which all Christian discipline must be guided. That is why the passage sounds so contemporary. Looking on a woman to lust after her is adultery of the heart in any country, century, or culture. The application to contemporary cases is direct. That is why when a Christian wife wants to divorce her non-Christian husband even though he desires to continue the marriage, a Christian counselor can say without qualification, "That would be sin; you cannot do it." In support of his assertion he may cite I Corinthians 7:13 and apply it directly.

However, there is another class of problems to which the Scriptures apply less directly. When a pastor must decide whether to reject a call to another church, when a young woman has to determine whether she will accept a proposal for marriage, and in hundreds of decisions (both large and small), the biblical principles must be brought to bear upon the question in such a way that they box in the number of possible answers. Such application of the Scriptures requires time, knowledge, and wisdom.[3]

One of the reasons why Christian counselors find themselves faced continually by counselees with myriad such questions is because many conservative pastors have failed to teach their members *how to use the Bible practically* to deal with such matters. They have taught (successfully) the factual study of the Bible—members from infancy, it seems, can recite verses and retrieve even esoteric biblical data for the next Bible quiz. Yet they do

[3]Cf. Archibald Alexander Hodge, *The Confession of Faith* (Reprint of 1869 ed.; London, 1964), p. 39.

not know how to consult the Bible helpfully in times of need or decision. I am certainly not against factual learning. But if learning never progresses beyond this to its practical (or *telic)* applications, it is not merely rendered useless, but positively harmful. Learning for its own sake leads to a kind of gnosticism in which the Bible becomes impractical for anything other than for argumentation. The Bible's use is limited to learning history and doctrine, or perhaps (at best) it may be used for moralizing. But as a Book to which one can turn for satisfying redemptive solutions to life problems—the Bible remains closed. When seminaries begin to teach pastors how to teach members of their congregations how to use the Bible for such purposes, the church will come to newness of life. Pastors who teach this way will save themselves and their members many heartaches and hours of unnecessary counseling.

At any rate, to begin with, *counselors* must learn how to use the Bible practically, and in the process they will find it necessary to teach counselees how to do so too.

A biblical plan of action that grows out of and at every point is consistent with biblical presuppositions, then, may do so either directly or indirectly. When Tom says, "I can't overcome my temper; I guess that Barb will just have to accept me as I am," the counselor may reply with confidence: "If you are truly a Christian, Tom, there is every hope that you can change, for the fruit of the Spirit is self-control. Barb should not accept you as you are since God doesn't." But when the counselor lays out a plan for Tom and Barb, *based on* the biblical principles taught in Ephesians 4:25-32, he may not speak at every point with quite the same authority. Instead, after a full discussion of the passage he may close like this: ". . . So, you see, there is hope. And the principles for putting off temper tantrums are clear—(1) daily communication rather than allowing the sun to go down on your anger; (2) words that build up and help another rather than tear him down; (3) forgiveness rather than slander, gossip, or malice. Now, let me suggest one way in which you can begin to put these principles into practice. If every day or so you meet to hold a conference. . . ," and so on. The counselor must distinguish clearly between the biblical *principles* and the suggested *plan* for putting those principles into action. The principles, if properly understood, are unalterable; the plan of implementation is negotiable. Principles must be applied; like dough and yeast, they must be worked into the actual problem situation. Yet, because situations differ, there may be many ways of doing so. It may be that regular use of a conference table will prove to be a vital part of the solution for Tom and Barb. On the other hand, different implementation of the same principles may be necessary for the counselor's very next case. The accomplished pianist learns basic principles and skills; after that he can play any piece, adapting his acquired abilities to the particular dimensions of each new tune.

But one thing is clear; in almost *every instance* of counseling success the one factor that seemed to make the difference was the implementation of biblical principles by means of a *concrete* plan of action. Without concrete application, the plan—no matter how biblical and wise (abstractly considered)—will fail. The biblical principles must be kneaded into the dough of the counselee's life.

Presumably it appears that while preachers and counselors are strong on the *what to,* they are weak on the *how to.* How often have we all preached abstractly: For example, "Don't read your Bible; study it." Enthusiastic members leave the service committed to remedying the defect. Monday they start in at Genesis 1:1, this time determined to study. By Thursday they have given up the task (since they didn't know *how to* do anything different from before). Sermons like that need to be accompanied by an announcement like this: ". . . and if you don't know how to study the Bible, be at church before the Sunday evening service when we shall begin a twelve-week course on the practical study of the Scriptures."

Counselors too need to keep in mind the fact that it is not enough to urge confused, undisciplined, disorganized, discouraged or hopeless people to stop unbiblical practices.[4] "How?" is the insistent question that they must be prepared to answer with a biblically grounded plan of implementation. But they must not wait for the counselee to articulate the question. Assuming that most counselees will be deficient not only about what-type material but also about the how-type, they will initiate the discussion themselves. Counselors, for example, will want to stock up on recommended devotional booklets to hand to couples who need to learn how to begin to read and pray together. They also may wish to devote some time to explaining some of the pitfalls to avoid and to making positive suggestions about time, method and regularity.

(2) But, secondly, a biblical plan of action aims at biblical goals. Christian counselors may not accept just *any* goal. That is one reason why the usual behavioristic approach to goal-setting cannot be adopted by Christian counselors. Behavioristic counselors, by and large, will take on counselees with the intention of helping them to meet any goals that counselees wish to set for themselves.[5] If a counselee wishes to learn how to make friends, keep a

---

[4]Counseling and preaching are complementary. Some advise, "Don't preach when you counsel." Why not? If one's preaching is good, it will have many characteristics in common with good counseling. The advice properly applies only to poor preaching.

[5]Cf. John D. Krumboltz, ed., *Revolution in Counseling* (Boston, 1966), pp. 9ff.

job, or become a good father, the Christian counselor knows that these goals must be discussed and shaped *from a scriptural viewpoint.* Consequently he will interpose questions like these: Should the counselee expect to keep a job, given his irresponsible behavior? Does he want to work for the glory of God? Can he be counseled adequately apart from an understanding and acceptance of the fundamental work ethic in Colossians 3:22-26, summed up in the words, "It is the Lord Christ whom you serve"? Such matters must be of uppermost concern to a Christian counselor. The *goals* of the counselee, then, must be discussed, evaluated, and often altered in the light of the Scriptures.

Moreover, goals cannot be abstracted from life styles and life commitments. Christian counselors (unlike behaviorists) must counsel the whole man. If, for example, a homosexual wishes to learn how to make a decision about his occupation, a behaviorist may work on that goal, feeling no compulsion to handle the problem of homosexuality. But Christian counselors cannot divorce the homosexual problem, or, for that matter, the more general problem of the counselee's relationship to Jesus Christ from the question of occupational choice. Phobias will be dealt with from a biblical stance—the fear of man will be related to biblical wisdom which begins with the fear of God. Problems may be isolated for analysis and worked on individually, but never out of context.

To continue, the Christian counselor, therefore, must use the Scriptures to evaluate and, thus, ultimately to determine every goal. Goals like integration, security, adaptation, and so forth, cannot be adopted uncritically. For instance, William Glasser, author of the well-known volume *Reality Therapy,* has written: "A normal being is one who functions effectively, has some degree of happiness, and achieves something worthwhile to himself

47

within the rules of the society in which he lives."[6] This definition of normality, the goal of Glasser's counseling, is faulty in several ways. But it must be rejected fundamentally, because it is humanistic, man-centered. Man is the goal setter and the evaluator. Each individual sets goals and evaluates according to his own subjective standards and the standards of others around him. Glasser, then, wants to please the counselee and at the same time to please society. No absolute objective standard is consulted. Consequently, the counselee is caught in the relativistic subjectivism of individual preferences, desires, and distortions of reality. Glasser thinks this is right so long as the individual can get away with being that way—or as he puts it: remains "within the rules of the society." That latter standard, the norms of the society, is no better than the former. For what cultural norms boil down to is this—Glasser wants to make the counselee to function smoothly within his society, whatever the rules of that society may be. If the counselee lives in a headhunting society, presumably Reality Therapy will help him to function effectively as a headhunter.

The Christian counselor should recognize that he can adopt neither the subjective standard of sinful individual desires nor the corporate standards of sinful societies as the goals or norms of counseling. He should realize that to make sinful man the standard is to set sinful goals for the counselee. He knows that God frequently requires Christians to set themselves *against* their own sinful desires and *against* the sinful norms of society. The faithful fathers of Hebrews 11 looked beyond themselves and away from society to the true and living God and to His heavenly city. They functioned according to another

[6]William Glasser, *Mental Health or Mental Illness?* (New York, 1970), p. 1.

set of standards—a heavenly one. Where did they get it? From God's Word. They believed His promises and lived by faith in accordance with His directives even though that frequently flung them headlong into conflict with those around them. So, it is clear that one's counseling is scriptural only when he sets scriptural goals and works toward them.

Ultimately all scriptural goals may be summed up in one goal: to glorify God. In doing so, with Paul, Christian counselors will seek to "present every man complete in Christ" (Col. 1:28). This may be accomplished by holding up before each counselee no less a goal than God's standard, namely "the fulness of Christ" (Eph. 4:13b). God is satisfied with nothing less than the goal of becoming like Him. But the only way that one can know what Christ is like is through the Scriptures.

(3) Next, a biblical plan of action depends upon biblical methods. Here is where many Christians founder. They can agree upon the need for biblical goals and objectives, "but," say they, "why can't we use any method that achieves the goal?" If Rogerian, Freudian, or Skinnerian methods are helpful in making a counselee more like Christ, then we shall use them.

In these post-Watergate days, it would seem superfluous to stress the fact that good ends do not justify questionable means. As a matter of fact, only means biblically justifiable can bring about biblical ends. Humanistic means cannot be employed in achieving Christian maturity. Freud knew nothing of means that would lead to Christlikeness. Rogerian methodology does not bring holiness. Skinnerian manipulation does not produce the fruit of the Spirit. Precisely because it is *His* fruit, the Holy Spirit's methods of fruit growing must be sought, found and used. And these can be found only in the Spirit's Book, the Bible.

I do not wish to labor this vital point, as I have dealt with it elsewhere in depth.[7] Instead, let me point out that it can only be with grave concern, therefore, that today we see the wholesale uncritical adoption of pagan methodologies by genuine Christians, who doubtless mean well and who hope thereby to reach the same goals as we. Yet, they are currently busily introducing (to the great injury of Christ's church) the methods of Encounter and Group Therapy, of Transactional Analysis, of Gestalt Therapy and of Behaviorism, just as they formerly uncritically brought Freudianism and Rogerianism into the church. We must resist this tendency to believe that means are unimportant. The ark of God must be borne on poles; it cannot be transported by oxcart.

(4) Finally, let me simply mention the fact that a biblical plan of action, though biblical in every other respect, may fail because it was sought and carried out from non-biblical motives. Biblical counselors will always be concerned about the motives of their counselees.

The area of motive is planted thickly with thorny questions. I shall mention but one. While, on the one hand, counselors must inquire about and discuss motives, on the other hand they are incapable of judging motives, for it is God alone who judges the "heart and the reins." Man looks only on the outward appearance. Having done their best to explain the proper biblical motivation behind the proposed plan of action, and having stressed the need for sincerity and warned against proceeding from lesser motivation, the counselor must prayerfully leave the outcome to God.[8]

Let us take an example. Pat, a professing Christian,

---

[7] Jay E. Adams, *The Christian Counselor's Manual*, pp. 5-8.
[8] Not implying, of course, that ultimately motivation may become known through life styles, and may even lead to church discipline: "By their fruit you will know them."

comes highly motivated to win back her husband, who has just left home and declares that he will never return. She begs, "I'll do anything to get Larry back! Just tell me what to do, please." The alert counselor will be wary of her *motives,* as well as her *objectives.* And if her words may be taken literally, when she says "I'll do anything. . . ," then he knows also that her strong desire would lead her to adopt biblical or non-biblical *methods* for achieving her end. He will soon bring the discussion around to goals and motives. He will say something like this: "Pat, as a Christian your goal must be to please God, regardless of the consequences. You must be willing to lose Larry if in the providence of God that should be the outcome. You cannot do what the Bible says simply as a technique or gimmick to get him back. It is true that if anything will bring Larry home again, it will be Christian behavior on your part, but you cannot make the changes that you must make primarily for that reason. You must be clear in your own mind that what God requires of you at this time must be done—*whether Larry returns or not.* You must do it out of genuine repentance and out of faith and love for God; because *He* says that this is what you must do. If Larry returns, then your secondary hope will be realized; but even if he doesn't, when your primary hope has been to please God, you will not be disappointed. Not only will you be what God wants you to be, but in His mercy you will realize His blessing to carry you through the midst of the trial. In no other way can you face the two possible outcomes with peace and assurance."

Counselees, then, should be instructed that at bottom the only scriptural motive for action is to please God. This leads very naturally to the next consideration.

CHAPTER VI
Working the Plan

Commitment to Scriptural Action by the Counselee

This is the fifth factor in the use of the Scriptures in counseling. Noble goals and motives, correct plans and procedures, while essential to any ensuing scriptural action on the part of the counselee, can never be substituted for it. He must become convicted by the Scriptures to make a commitment to take this biblical course of action.

Commitment to the biblical plan of action is, of course, altogether essential, for unless the counselee actually does what God requires, all else will have been in vain. Exposition, conviction of sin, understanding and even belief that this plan is biblical and would succeed, all will have been useless if he does not in fact follow it. "Why wouldn't he do so if he saw all of that?" you may wonder. Well listen to four common responses with which every counselor is familiar:

"I can't."

"I won't."

"It would be too embarrassing."

"I'm afraid."

When a counselee has confessed his sin of gossip to God and sought forgiveness, he may be faced with the need to apologize to the persons about whom he spread the gossip. Any one of the four above replies may be forthcoming. The counselor must be prepared to meet each, scripturally of course.

"I can't" may be interpreted in at least two ways: (1) it

would be too hard; (2) I don't know how to do it. The latter response may be handled in a number of ways. For instance, by using a scriptural model ("Here is how Paul faced trouble. Let's look at Philippians 1"); the concreteness needed can be emphasized by the selection of a concrete passage. Or the counselor may take the principle and apply it directly in a concrete fashion: "Since you must not let the sun go down on your anger, it will be necessary for you to see Brad right away."

If by "can't" he means, "It would be too hard" or "I simply don't have what it takes," the counselor can give strong assurance from the scriptures that God never calls upon His children to do that which they cannot do by His strength. Using the line of argument from I Corinthians 10:13 suggested in my pamphlet, *Christ and Your Problems,* he can both give hope and press the counselee's responsibility upon him. Sometimes "I can't" at first seems to mean "It would be too hard," but in reality turns out to mean "I don't know how." That, naturally, can be a good reason for thinking the task is too hard. The counselor should be alert to all of the possibilities.

But suppose the response is "I won't." Here again at least two possibilities exist. Often, recalcitrant counselees, because of the perverseness of sinful human nature, balk just before they give in. Automobile salesmen call this the kicking-the-tires routine. Counselors will encounter it frequently enough to become aware of it. Firm continued insistence upon the biblical principle, leaving the counselee with the responsibility to do as God requires after prayer for help, often will be rewarded. Once the Word of God has been presented clearly and conviction is present, resistance soon may break down. The counselee will report that between the sessions he did what he had intended not to do—and frequently—on the very next day.

"I won't," however, may be indicative of a more serious problem. Actual rebellious resistance may lie behind the reply. In such cases, after a reasonable amount of time to determine whether, in fact, the problem is rebellion or some other, if the counselor is convinced upon sufficient grounds that there is an unwillingness to accept the authority of Jesus Christ in the Scriptures, he must warn the counselee (and be prepared to back up the warning if necessary) that such rebellion against Christ can lead only to church discipline. If adequate warning is met with a stiffnecked response, the actual process of discipline must be instituted, hopefully leading at length to repentance and the fruits appropriate to repentance, but if not, revealing what can only be interpreted by the church as such serious rejection of the authority of Christ as to force the elders of the congregation to expel him for this and to look on him "as a heathen and a publican."

The response, "It would be too embarrassing," must be met with gentle firmness. "Of course, it will be embarrassing; I did not say that it would be easy or pleasant," the counselor may reply. He may continue, "Sin always leads to embarrassment—now or later. How much better to deal with it now; remove the offending thorn and be over and done with it. Then you will not have to go on with the threat of embarrassment and the guilt of your sin continually before you." To reinforce this biblical principle, the counselor may refer to Psalm 32, which David wrote in order to encourage Christians to deal with sin quickly. In it he explained his own misery occasioned by delay. Concluding the Psalm he warns not to be stubborn like the horse or mule that must be dragged to confession.

"I'm afraid," may call for much the same approach, but, if the fear is severe or complicated, may also demand a challenge to Christian courage that goes beyond. A reminder that Christians have not been given "a spirit of timidity, but of power and love and discipline" (II Tim. 1:7) will need to be given: "The Holy Spirit will give you power to overcome your fear through love and discipline." John says, "Mature love casts our fear" (I John 4:18). "You must show your love for God by doing what He requires in spite of your fears. Prayerfully discipline yourself to do this task by submitting closely to the Word of God, and you will be able to overcome the most fearful problem, no matter what it may be. Once you have torn yourself away from your feeling of fear, to obey God, you will discover that the fear will lessen or disappear altogether, since a large part of fear is the fear of experiencing the feeling of fear itself."[1]

When a counselee commits himself to a biblical plan of action, it may be well for the counselor to check out carefully precisely what the counselee intends to do and how. If, for instance, he is to seek forgiveness from another, it might be well to ask the counselee to tell him in a dry run just about what he will say and how. If he will do so in a letter, then the counselee might be encouraged to bring in a rough draft for evaluation before writing and mailing the final copy. Suggestions for saying it differently or changing a phrase or two in the letter may make a great difference.

The counselor will be aware of possible pitfalls and warn against these. The counselee may plan to say, "Joe, I came to apologize for my nasty response toward you when you pulled that dirty financial deal on me." The counselor will point out that this will not do, for the

---

[1]Indeed, when one out of love for God and/or neighbor does what the Scriptures require *regardless of the consequences* ("If I panic, I panic. It will be rough, but I'll survive."), for the first time he begins to free himself of fear. Fearing fear brings fear. It is like a self-fulfilling prophecy. Not trying to stop the fear experience stops it.

counselee is mixing accusations with apology. He will help him to see that first he must remove the log from his own eye, and that only after that matter is dealt with and forgiveness has been received can the other question be raised separately at a subsequent point. Moreover, the counselor will note that emotionally-laden words like "dirty deal" serve only to incite wrath rather than bring about reconciliation.

And finally, when commitments to hard tasks are made, it is wise frequently (especially when the counselee is reluctant or afraid) to ask him to suggest and agree upon an early date when he plans to do it. Abraham "arose early" to sacrifice his son Isaac. This was probably the most unpleasant task to which he had ever been called. So. . . he got right to it, as soon as possible. The longer a difficult assignment is delayed, the more likely we are to worry about it, making the task seem all the more formidable and finding that we are less able to comply.

In conclusion, then, the counselee must be helped to formulate and to carry out a biblical plan of action. But even when he does, he may not then say to God, "I'm OK; You're OK," for, as we shall see in the next chapter, all of the credit, all of the glory, all of the honor must go to neither the counselee nor the counselor, but to the Spirit of the living God, who by His Word and power has *at every point* been the One who enabled the counseling to reach a successful end.

CHAPTER VII
The Spirit and the Scriptures

We have seen how the Scriptures must permeate Christian counseling from start to finish. The counselee's problem can be understood christianly only as it is evaluated biblically. The solution to his problem, likewise, must be found in the Scriptures. How the latter is applied to the former, how a concrete plan of action may be formulated and carried out—all of these steps in counseling are dependent upon the Scriptures.

When a Christian comes to his pastor for help, therefore, he should expect him to offer help, like the Levite, from the Scriptures. God Himself said: "For the lips of a priest should keep knowledge, and men should seek the law from his mouth, because he is the messenger of the Lord of hosts" (Mal. 2:7; cf. also Nah. 8:7-9). There should be no question, then, for either the counselee or the counselor over whether the counsel that the Lord's messenger gives should be scriptural counsel. To be obedient to God, the New Testament minister can do no less than his Old Testament predecessor.

But there is another angle from which this matter may be approached. The reason why Christian counseling depends so heavily upon the Scriptures at every point is because the Scriptures are the peculiar product of the Counselor Himself. When I say that the Counselor Himself is the Author of the Scriptures, I refer, of course, not to the human counselor, but to the Holy Spirit, who is called by John "the paraclete" (counselor) and by Isaiah "the Spirit of Counsel" (Isa. 11:2). He is the Spirit by

57

whom God breathed out His Words in written form in the Scriptures, the One who patiently spent long years bearing along men of God that by His holy superintendence they might write inerrant counsel. It should be no surprise, then, to find that He works through the Bible when carrying out His paracletic functions. This, as a matter of fact, is precisely what Paul asserted in Romans 15:4 when he explained: "For whatever was written in earlier times was written for our instruction, that through perseverance and the *paraclesis* of the Scriptures we might have hope." Just a few verses later (v. 13) he added: "Now may the God of hope fill you with all joy and peace in believing, that you may abound in hope by the power of the Spirit." Hope, Paul at first says, comes from the Scriptures, but then he claims that hope comes from the Holy Spirit. There is no contradiction. Paul has no difficulty in sometimes identifying the source of this paracletic work as the Spirit and at other times as the Scriptures since it is *by means of the Scriptures* that the Spirit counsels.

The interchange of such terminology in speaking of books and authors is well known even among ourselves. We may say with equal ease and without occasioning the slightest misunderstanding, "The source of the quotation is C. S. Lewis" or "The source is *The Lion, the Witch and the Wardrobe.*" Thus, in a similar sense, but with further qualification respecting the human agency that was involved in the writing of the Bible, an Old Testament quotation may be introduced with the words "The Holy Spirit, by the mouth of our father David, said. . ." (Acts 4:25; cf. also Acts 1:16; Heb. 3:7).

So, to begin with, we must be aware of the fact that the counsel of the Holy Spirit is closely connected with the Scriptures. Indeed, that counsel is identical with, and found only in, the pages of the Bible. That is why Paul can speak of the *paraclesis* (or counsel) of the Scriptures.

Recognition of this identification is fundamental to all Christian counseling. The fact should influence both the counselor and the counselee to a significant degree. The attitude of the counselor must be confidence and relief: "I do not have to *counsel alone;* when I counsel biblically, I use divine truth and the Holy Spirit has promised to work through my counseling." On the other side of the desk, the counselee also may rejoice in the fact that he does not have to *change alone;* indeed he knows that he cannot. When he walks in God's will, it is because he walks "in (or by) the Spirit"; when he begins to love, show self-control, enjoy peace, and so forth, he acknowledges that he did not produce these blessings himself. With Paul he calls them the "fruit (i.e., the product) of the Spirit." Both must come to see what, in Ezekiel's prophecy points to the central fact: "I will put my Spirit within you and cause you to *walk in my statutes"* (Ezek. 36:27). Thus He promises to enable Christians to *learn* and to *live* according to God's revealed will.

As a matter of fact, it is the Holy Spirit who accomplishes each of these things for both the counselor and the counselee:

1. He illuminates the believer's mind so that he can interpret the Scriptures, giving ability to understand and wisdom to know how to live according to the will of God. This He does as *the Spirit of truth* (John 14:17; 15:26; 16:13) *and of wisdom* (Isa. 11:2; I Cor. 2:13).

2. He gives power both to will and to do that will of God whenever believers step out by faith in obedience to scriptural injunctions (Ezek. 36:27). This He does as *the Spirit of holiness* (Rom. 1:4).

The Spirit, then, gives power to *know* and power to *do*. This twofold work of the Spirit is vital, for the counselor must *know* the truth of God in order to counsel and, as we have seen, he must have courage to *say and do* as God wishes in spite of opposition or strong temptations to veer from the scriptural course. Likewise, the counselee needs to *learn* of his condition and what God requires him to do about it; he then needs strength and patience to *effect* the needed changes. The Spirit, through His Word, provides all that is required to meet these needs. In scriptural counseling the Spirit works—as He wills—on both sides of the counseling desk; He comes at the problem from each end; He works in the counselor and in the counselee.

Let us now reconsider one or two of the five factors mentioned previously to see how the Holy Spirit brings each of these into play in counseling by means of the Scriptures. Those factors were:

1. a biblical understanding of the counselee's problem, stemming from. . .

2. a clear recognition of the Holy Spirit's purpose in scriptural passages appropriate to both the problem and the solution, and. . .

3. a meeting of man's problem and God's full solution in counseling, according to. . .

4. the formulation of a biblical plan of action, leading toward. . .

5. commitment to scriptural action by the counselee.

Consider, for example, the first factor: *A biblical understanding of the counselee's problem.* It is the work of the Holy Spirit to bring conviction of sin (John 16:8); it is also the function of the Scriptures to do so (James 2:9: "convicted by the law as a transgressor"). Again, there is no contradiction: the Holy Spirit does His convicting work *by means of* the Scriptures. In his second letter to young Timothy, Paul directs him to "preach the Word" (II Tim. 4:2). In explanation he continues: "reprove, rebuke, exhort." The word "reprove" actually is the term that elsewhere is translated "convict." In Titus 1:9, Paul wrote ". . . holding fast the faithful word which is in accordance with the teaching, that he may be able. . . to convict"; and in Titus 2:15, he urged, "These things speak and exhort and convict with all authority." Plainly, in these passages concerning "conviction," it is not Timothy or Titus who "convicts"; it is the Holy Spirit. But it is equally evident that He uses the human preacher or counselor as His agent and the Scriptures as the means for bringing about conviction.

There can be no true understanding of a problem in living, then, unless the Holy Spirit enables the counselee to see himself in that Word as in a mirror and, thereby, convicts him of his sin. Every such problem is plainly described (not projected) there. The Holy Spirit enables the counselee to see sin as sin—as rebellion against God by the transgression of His law. But since behavior can be identified as sin only when evaluated by God's standard, counselors must employ the Scriptures if they would seek to bring counselees to an understanding of the true nature of their problems, and if they would have them to be motivated to do as God says. As Paul put it, "I would not have come to know sin except through the law" (Rom. 7:7). Therefore, all modern attempts to understand man's problem fail, for while sin brings about alienation or estrangement, it cannot be *equated* with alienation or estrangement. While sin leads to poor patterns of learning and maladaptation, it cannot be *equated* with failure to learn or adapt. While sin disorients one toward life, that is not its essential feature. Problems in living can be understood properly only when the basic dimension of sin as rebellion against God through lawlessness is seen in them; and there is absolutely no reason to expect this to happen unless the Holy Spirit enables one to understand

61

his problem in the light of the Scriptures. Whenever the Spirit gives such understanding, it leads to conviction.

Thus, it is accurate to say that when a Christian counselee has a biblical understanding of his problem, he is not merely able to tag it or to label it scripturally; rather, for him to understand the problem biblically is for him to become convicted over the fact that fundamentally his problem is with God. Such conviction comes only from the Holy Spirit working by His Word.

But we have seen that the Holy Spirit not only helps the counselee, He also helps the counselor. In bringing counsel to His church, the Holy Spirit has chosen to work through those in whom the Word of Christ "dwells richly" (Col. 3:16), or as Paul noted elsewhere: by those who are "filled with all knowledge and able to confront one another nouthetically" (Rom. 15:14). Such knowledge and wisdom come, as I Corinthians 2 makes clear, from the Holy Spirit. So from each side of the counseling context, both the counselor's scriptural knowledge and wisdom, through which the Holy Spirit prepares him to give biblical counsel, and the counselee's biblical understanding of the problem leading to conviction of sin and repentance, are the result of the work of the Holy Spirit using the Scriptures. Neither counselor nor counselee can take credit for anything productive that comes from counseling; it is always the "fruit of the Spirit."

Thus, the Holy Spirit always must be acknowledged to be the Spirit of counsel, the Spirit of truth, the Spirit of wisdom, and the Spirit of holiness. The use of the genitive in each of these descriptions of the Spirit shows Him to be the *source* of these blessings. All knowledge of God and of what His children may do to please Him is the result of the Spirit's bringing knowledge and understanding with conviction through His Word.

CHAPTER VIII
The Spiritual Struggle in Counseling

But it is not enough to know God's Word, to be convicted of sin and to repent. How does scriptural counseling prevent sinful behavior and attitudes for the future? The greatest problem with which Christians struggle is in obeying the directive: "The things you have learned and received and heard and seen in me, practice these things; and the God of peace shall be with you" (Phil. 4:9). It is one thing to hear the truth, to know the truth, to see it in practice—and even to be convicted about one's failures and what God wants done to meet them—it is quite another to "walk in the truth." How does the Spirit "cause" one to "walk" in God's "statutes" (Ezek. 36:27)? To put it another way, how can the struggle against the "desire of the flesh" mentioned in Galatians 5:16 be waged successfully? This is the fundamental problem of counseling—to effect change that sticks. A brief consideration of the passage in Galatians may help.

First, notice the "flesh sets its desire *against* the Spirit and the Spirit against the flesh" (v. 17). The two, Paul continues, are "in opposition to one another." And, note, it is because of this fleshly opposition that "you may not do the things that you please" (v. 17). The "things that you please," here, refers to those things that Christians, *as Christians* wish to do to please God.

At least three questions that are pertinent to counseling leap from the text:

(1) What is the "flesh" mentioned in these verses?

(2) Generally, how may one overcome the desire of the flesh?

(3) Specifically, how is this accomplished in the counseling context?

The First Question

What is "flesh?" Much study has been given to the question of Paul's use of the term "flesh." Beyond the ordinary uses of this word in the writings of Paul and other authors, it is well known that there is a peculiar Pauline usage that occurs primarily (though not exclusively; cf. Rom. 13:14; Eph. 2:3) in these verses in Galatians and in Romans, chapters 7-8. In each of these passages, flesh is set in antithesis to something else. A study of the term in such antithetical usage yields the following information. On the one hand, "flesh" is set in contrast to the *Spirit*, to the new *mind* given by Christ and to the *inner man*. On the other hand, "flesh" is identified with *the old man, the body of sin*, the *mortal body*, the *members of the body*, the *body of this death*, the *deeds of the body*, the *former manner of life, sin that indwells, sin in the members*, and *evil that is present in me*.

One thing seems evident; in the struggle the opposing forces are clearly identified. Let us consider the enemies. Against the flesh are arrayed the Spirit (i.e., the Holy Spirit) and the Christian, who in Christ has a new *mind* and who in his *inner man*, (i.e., in his deepest desires) wishes to please God and to overthrow the flesh. The struggle is carried on within the believer. But the deeds of the flesh are also something for which the believer is responsible. These are the fulfillment of the desire of the flesh. The "desire of the flesh," or the "evil that is present in me," or the "sin in my members," however, can be counteracted rather than carried into effect (Gal. 5:16) so that "the desire of the flesh" need not issue in "the deeds of the flesh."

Did Paul believe in a Greek dualism in which the fleshly

body was set over against the soul, the former being evil and the latter holy? Is that what we are confronted with here? Absolutely not. Christianity came into a Greek world with a message that scandalized the Greeks precisely because Christian preachers taught that the body was not essentially evil but good and that, indeed, it would be fully redeemed at the resurrection. The incarnation of Christ forever puts the lie to all Greek or Gnostic notions that there is a body/soul, evil/good cleavage. Christian anthropology always has resisted any such dualistic ideas.

But because some theologians (rightly) feared dualistic notions in which the body might be declared to be evil *per se,* they (wrongly) shied away from the obvious import of Paul's words when he spoke of sin in the flesh. "Flesh" in such passages, they contended, must refer to something other than the fleshly body. Hence, by some the word was conveniently equated with "self"; by others it was said to be used in a purely "ethical" sense. Whichever way one went, he always was careful to strip away from the term any direct corporeal reference.

One can only laud the desire to defeat dualism that led to these interpretations, but the desire grew out of fear and, alas, led to another problem—how could the "flesh" be dealt with when it was merely an ethical concept or when it represented a self which was not identical to the "inner man" or the "mind" of the believer? The battle too often became an abstract concept that was out of reach rather than the crucial life factor with which every believer must grapple.

Of great significance in this discussion is the fact that, in spite of everything, *flesh* does have as its primary referent the corporeal. That fundamental feature cannot be removed so facilely. Look, for instance, at its synonyms and associations: the *body* of sin, the mortal *body,* the *members* of the *body,* the deeds of the *body,* the *body* of this death, sin in the *members* (of the *body),* and so forth. Surely, in such company as it keeps, "flesh," even here, *must* be understood to refer to the corporeal unless there are stronger reasons, than to date have been forthcoming, to divest it of such content. Note also that flesh is contrasted with the *inner man.* While the term *outer man* is not used, it clearly is implied.[1] What is the contrast to *inner man* if it is not the body?

Does that not leave us with a dualism then? No, not at all; rather it presents us with an antithesis and an antagonism. That such an antithesis is in view in Galatians 5 and in Romans 6-8 everyone agrees. There is an antithesis on the one hand, between the Spirit and the inner man that He is renewing, and on the other hand, the believer's body *as it is still wrongly habituated.*[2]

"Flesh" as Paul uses it in a negative sense, then, means just that: a body habituated to the ways of the world rather than to the ways of God. The idea of bodily habituation appears frequently in the pertinent contexts. The *flesh* is the "former manner of life" or "previous habits" also referred to as the "old man" in Ephesians 4:22. It is the "old man with his *practices*" in Colossians 3:9.[3] It is the sinful ways that have been programmed and patterned into life by our sinful natures through continuous yielding of the "members" of the body to sin (Rom. 6:13,19). Before salvation, the Christian was a willing slave who offered the members of his body as instruments to carry out the wishes of his master, sin. Now, with the same willingness, he must learn to yield the members of his body to God.

---

[1]And, in Rom. 2:28 the phrase "outward in the flesh'" does occur.
[2]Including the brain.
[3]Note, *praxis,* a manner, practice, or way of life, is used; not merely *ergon,* a deed.

The power of habit is great. It is not easy to please God in a body that is still in part habituated to sin. Though he may wish inwardly to cease lying, to control his tongue, to stop losing his temper, or to eliminate scores of other vices, the believer finds that the battle against the habituated desires of the body is hard. There are victories, but they do not come easily. Indeed, in his own strength he will fail to win the struggle. But that is not the dismal conclusion of the matter, for Paul both in Galatians and in Romans plainly points to the way to victory. And this fact leads us to a consideration of the next point.

The Second Question

Generally speaking, how may one overcome the desire of the flesh? Paul's answer is explicit: "Walk by the Spirit, and you will not carry out the desire of the flesh" (Gal. 5:16). Two verses later (v. 18) he speaks of this walk as Spirit "led." Moreover, in Romans 8:13-14, he affirms: "If you are living according to the flesh, you must die; but if by the Spirit you are putting to death the deeds of the body you will live. For all who are being led by the Spirit of God, these are the sons of God."

The Scriptures are unequivocal: it is the Spirit of God who, in opposition to the flesh, leads the believer into a new way of life. Christian counseling therefore requires the Spirit's leading work. We must consider this leading in some detail, however, for again leading is not what it often (superficially) has been claimed to be.

What is the leading of the Spirit, and how does it take place? The answer to that question is: it is a leading into the new ways of the new life, into the paths of righteousness; it is leading that occurs in obedience to the Scriptures. It is the same as Ezekiel's "causing to walk" in God's "statutes."

When a counselee says, "But I don't feel led. . .," the

counselor must point out to him that in so using such a phrase he is not speaking biblically, for there are only two passages in which the leading of the Spirit is mentioned (Rom. 8:1-15; Gal. 5:16-18), and in neither of these does leading have anything to do with guidance in decision making through feelings. Rather, in these passages the Christian is identified as one who is led by the Spirit into a new life pleasing to God. The stress in this leading is upon the power that He provides to produce a new *way* of life. For instance, in Romans 8 the preceding thirteen verses pertain to the Christian life, which is described as a "walk according to the Spirit" (v. 4), a "mind set on the Spirit" (v. 6), "being in the Spirit" (v. 9) and "living" according to the Spirit (v. 12). Indeed, being Spirit "led" is closely connected with "putting to death the deeds of the body by the Spirit" (v. 13). A son of God, then, is one who, by the shepherdly work of the Spirit, is led in the paths of righteousness. He is one who is being led to walk in new ways by putting to death the sinful habit practices of the old man, and who in their place, is producing the fruit of the Spirit. In short, what Paul says is that you can tell who is a believer by observing the process of sanctification at work within him. You know the Spirit is present in those in whom His work is evident.

In Galatians 5:16, Paul commands, "Walk by the Spirit and you will not carry out the desire of the flesh." It is the Spirit who effectively enables the believer to keep the desire of the flesh (that is, the sinful responses that the body is programmed, and therefore desires, or finds easy, to express) from issuing into the "deeds of the flesh." This he does by leading him into new habit patterns appropriate to the new walk of a child of God. Another way to put it is to say that the believer is led to produce the "fruit of the Spirit."

The process of sanctification is always in view when

Paul writes of the Spirit leading. There is not the slightest idea of special revelation, impressions and feelings or any other subjective method of guidance under consideration. Rather, in both passages the power of the Spirit that enables the believer to overcome the desire of the flesh and to learn new patterns of life is the subject of His leading. This fact moves us to the consideration of the third question.

The Third Question

Specifically, how does the Spirit enable the believer to win battles with the flesh? The answer to this lies in a matter vital to all counseling that only can be mentioned here, but is developed fully elsewhere.[4] The child's joke:

Question: When is a door not a door?

Answer: When it is ajar.

may be devoid of humor but serves well as a model for an important biblical principle that is basic to Christian counseling. Think of the joke this way:

Question: When is a door not a door?

Answer: When it has become *something else.*

What the paradigm shows is that change in counseling is not a single, but rather a two-factored process. That means that the Spirit deals with the flesh by enabling the believer to do two things.

Let's look at an example or two. A counselee has a problem overcoming habits of lying. Since becoming a Christian, he knows that lying displeases God, and he wants to stop. Yet, in spite of good intentions and prayerful effort, he discovers that whenever heavy pressures are exerted upon him, he "automatically" lies. Sometimes the lies are out of his mouth before he even

---

[4]Jay Adams, *The Christian Counselor's Manual,* chaps. 14-15.

recognizes that he has uttered them. The body has been programmed by long-standing practice to lie as an escape from such stresses and—faithful to all past training—thus it responds. The flesh has won again. What can be done to deal with the flesh?

Take another example. Perhaps the counselee is a Christian who has a record of stealing. He, too, finds that the temporary cessation of his former practices is not sufficient to erase the pattern itself. How does he overcome the desire of the flesh? What of drug addicts, drunkards, homosexual sinners, and a host of others who have found that it is not easy simply to quit, even when one has good intentions? How can they be helped?

The Christian counselor remembers the model:

Question: When is a thief not a thief?

When is a liar not a liar?

Is the answer: "When he stops stealing?" or "When he stops lying?" No! That is a faulty, unbiblical single-factored answer that is bound to lead to failure. Instead, the biblical counselor remembers Ephesians 4 and Colossians 3, in which Paul insists that the "former manner of life" and the "practices" of the old man can be changed only by putting on *as well as* putting off. When a liar tries to stop lying, he is only doing part of what God requires. A liar who stops lying is still a liar who (at the moment) happens not to be lying; a thief who stops stealing is simply a thief who is between jobs.

Well, then, when is a liar not a liar; when is a thief not a thief? Answer: "When he has become something else." Specifically, what? Paul wrote: "Therefore, laying aside falsehood, speak truth each one of you with his neighbor, for we are members of one another" (Eph. 4:25). Well, then,

Question: When is a liar not a liar?

70

Answer: When he has become a truth teller—and not before.

He also wrote: "Let him who steals steal no longer; but rather let him labor, performing with his own hands what is good, in order that he may have something to share with him who has need" (Eph. 4:28). So, then,

Question: When is a thief not a thief?

Answer: When he has become a steady worker who shares with those in need.

And so it goes.

The Spirit leads not only *out of* but also *into;* by His power the believer can learn to resist the desire of the flesh and put to death the "deeds of the body" (Rom. 8:13), and in its place to produce the fruit of the Spirit. He reprograms him for righteousness. To the extent that this fruit is present the flesh cannot prevail, for it has been preempted by new patterns. After cataloging the fruit of the Spirit, Paul asserts: "Against such things there is no law." The works of the flesh are condemned by the Law; it is against the flesh. But the Spirit's fruit is the fulfillment of the Law.

Thus, the Christian counselor aims at effecting change that is permanent; change in which new ways replace old ones. Apart from the two-factored, biblical change just described, counselees will remain caught in the kiss-and-make-up syndrome. He knows that such change alone is adequate because God says so. Moreover, he knows that apart from the Scriptures this sort of change is not possible, for it is in the Scriptures alone that he can find God's alternatives to the old sinful patterns. He will not rest, therefore, until God's new ways have been introduced into the counselee's life and have begun to replace the old ones.

These changes, note, involve *biblical alternatives*. In II Timothy 3, mentioned at the outset, you will recall that

Paul listed four uses that the Scriptures play in a believer's life:

they teach, they convict, they correct,

and. . . they *train in righteousness*. Not only do they tell us what God requires, how we have failed and what we can do to get right with God again; they also provide all that is necessary to enable us to learn how to live a new way of life that glorifies God. We do not have to be everlastingly working on the same problem. By God's grace we can make progress; we can move on to the next.

From start to finish, counseling is the work of the Spirit of God. He provides the direction and He provides the power. The ways and means, as well as the goals, equally are presented in the Scriptures. The Spirit of God works through His Word to change men. May He thus work through you as you minister that Word in Christ's Name!

CHAPTER IX

The Application of the Scriptures to Specific Problems

In this chapter I should like further to unpack some of the principles enunciated earlier. While I hope that, in general, I have illustrated the practical use of the Scriptures *throughout* fully enough to be clear, nevertheless, since there is so much poor use of Scriptures it seems advisable to demonstrate the process once again in a few more instances. Briefly, therefore, I shall take up some specific situations and try to show how the Scriptures may be used in meeting concrete problems associated with each.

In order to do so, I shall turn to several of the cases set forth in *The Christian Counselor's Casebook*[1] (q.v.) and attempt to apply the foregoing principles and practices to them. I shall not discuss these cases in full, but shall focus merely upon one aspect of them—how the counselor might have used the Scriptures at some point or points in each case.

Now, first let us turn to a case in which it should be clear that the influence of the Scriptures upon the counselor must be all-determinative. In this case, you will notice that there are several problems. However, I should like to isolate but one.

---

[1]Jay Adams, *The Christian Counselor's Casebook* (Presbyterian & Reformed Pub. Co., Nutley: 1974). This study book contains 140 cases in workbook form.

"The Pistol is at My Head"

Your telephone rings one morning at one o'clock, and you find yourself speaking with Mary, a middle-aged married woman, the mother of two teenagers, who, together with her family, is a member of your congregation: You have noticed that she has missed services recently, but you had no other indication of any difficulty. However, there is no doubt in your mind as you listen to her now that she has been drinking heavily, and worse yet, she is threatening to commit suicide. You talk, trying to get the story. Her response to your questions about how she expects to take her life is both swift and frightening: "The pistol is at my head as I speak." You urge Mary to talk over her problem, assuring her that the situation indeed is serious and should get immediate attention. But, she refuses to tell you anything more unless you swear never to reveal to anyone what she tells you.

(Case I - 1, pp. 2,3)

Obviously, this is not a full counseling situation. Indeed, it is essential for the pastor not to try to counsel under such conditions. In role playing this case trainees often attempt to counsel over the phone. That is exactly the wrong thing to do. Mary is drunk; and the counselor must recognize that it is virtually impossible to counsel her while she is intoxicated. Secondly, she is making demands which must be overcome before it is possible to do effective counseling—she wants a commitment to absolute silence. Thirdly, the immediate crisis issue is to get her to put down the gun; nothing else. The counselor should not allow himself to be moved away from that fact. It is central.

I shall not go into all of the factors that might indicate

that this is a precounseling rather than a counseling situation, nor shall I discuss other interesting aspects of the case. All that I wish to note here is that the Scriptures must control the counselor at every point. In this instance, unless the counselor has a scriptural orientation, it is likely that he will go astray. I am referring specifically to the demand for confidentiality. The Christian counselor, in contrast to others, does not accept the premise that all information must be kept confidential; from time to time he may have to warn various counselees that what they are about to reveal he may not be able to keep in confidence. For example, he may not accept privileged information in confidence (for more on this, see *The Christian Counselor's Manual*[2]). And in this situation, he again is aware of the direct bearing of the Bible upon Mary's request. Passages like Proverbs 12:13 and 20:25, that condemn rash vows, should make him wary of acceding to her request and giving his word to Mary. If she has committed an illegal act that should be revealed, he must for her sake, as well as for the welfare of society be free to reveal it if sufficient encouragement over a period of time does not induce her to do so herself. I shall not discuss how the counselor may go about dealing with Mary's demand; obviously there are several things that he may do. But the crucial fact is that in meeting the demand he must think *scripturally*. Thus his approach will take either the route of avoiding the issue entirely, if possible (it is difficult to reason with a drunk), or of postponement till a later point (He may say: "Mary, you can trust me to do what the Bible tells me to do," or "Mary, this is too important a matter to discuss on the phone; I'm coming over. I'll talk to you about it then," etc.). Thus, concern for scriptural fidelity motivates him even in a time of extreme crisis. Indeed, any lesser orientation might open

[2]Pp. 269, 270.

him to every sort of dangerous and God-dishonoring practice. It is a heavy reliance upon the Scriptures that carries the counselor through crises successfully. It is hard to act in a crisis apart from structure and well-defined principle.

"I Want to Punch Her"

"Yes, this is probably the heart of it," Louise says to the counselor. "My heart *is* filled with bitterness toward Mildred."

"Now has your friend done something to elicit this reaction?" the counselor inquires.

"Well, she always butts her nose into our family affairs. We've been having some trouble with Jeff, our 17-year-old son. And we've been seeking guidance from the Lord. But Mildred seems to think that *she* has *all* the answers. She's always saying, you shouldn't do this, you shouldn't do that, you'd better do this, you'd better do that, and on and on. Sometimes I just feel like screaming. I almost want to punch her at times! She makes me *so* mad!"

"Yes, I can see that. I know that your reaction is a natural one. Most parents are defensive when they are criticized by outsiders. But you have to see something, Louise. Letting the bitterness build up is unhealthy for you. You should try to rid yourself of it. As you have already found out, it only results in increasing your frustration."

(Case II - 14, pp. 150,151)

This case is a good example of the sort of situation in which the counselor failed because he took less than a scriptural approach to the problem. The counselor encourages Louise to talk negatively about Mildred behind her back in direct violation of Ephesians 4:31, which forbids slanderous talk, and James 4:11 which commands: "Do not speak against *(katalaleo,* which means to speak negatively against someone behind his back) a brother, brethren." Moreover, this counselor calls sinful behavior "natural" (in a good sense), thus excusing her sin, and speaks humanistically only of the consequences of her behavior for herself (God's concerns are ignored). Also, he encourages blameshifting (he indicates that Louise's behavior is the direct result of Mildred's failures). Clearly, this pastor either does not have a biblical orientation at all or he has accommodated himself to a psychological orientation.

The biblical pastor, keeping the previously mentioned passages in mind, as a guide for his own approach, might do well to introduce Romans 12:14-21 into the counseling session as a base for helping Louise to solve her problems biblically. Without spelling out the way in which the pastor might have confronted Louise (see information in *The Christian Counselor's Manual* for this), it should be evident that this portion of the Scriptures is pertinent to the problem at hand. In that passage, Paul sorts out the responsibilities; "so far as it depends upon you" (v. 18), puts an end to excuses, allows for no retaliation (vv. 18-20), prohibits blame-shifting, ("do not be overcome by evil" v. 21), and again and again insists that in spite of the poor behavior of others God holds the believer responsible for returning good for evil (vv. 14,17,20,21). The counselor in the *Casebook* failed because he viewed the problem in the same way that Louise did. He was not coming to the problem with the "Word of Christ dwelling richly within" (Colossians 3:16). Because his viewpoint was as unscriptural as hers, he could not help her. Louise needed to be confronted with an antithetical, godly viewpoint; the last thing that she needed was more of the same. True empathy does not necessitate agreement of viewpoint, but rather concern deep enough to disagree.

Other passages that might have been used as the session progressed are Ephesians 4:26,29,31,32 and I Corinthians 13:4-7.[3] Because I have written extensively about Ephesians 4 elsewhere, I shall not say more about that passage. Rather, let me at least note how the latter passage may be applied. Louise had interpreted Mildred's words and actions in the worst possible light. Love would demand, however, that they be interpreted in the best light (cf. I Corinthians 13:7, "believes all things, hopes all things"). The counselor, instead of calling her bitterness "natural" ought to call it sinful, and should point out to Louise that God has obligated her to put the best construction upon Mildred's advice. In that way, even annoying behavior can be looked upon in terms of the good intentions possibly underlying it, thus allowing for a better relationship to develop in spite of differences of opinion or of personality. It is interesting that those who in the name of empathy (as a matter of fact true empathy demands something quite different) simply agree with a counselee soon find that agreement means that there is no further advice that can be given since they see the problem as the counselee does. There is nothing to do to help when one thinks that the counselee is already doing all that can be expected of him. The fact is that bringing the biblical viewpoint to bear upon the situation always offers a counseling alternative to the counselee's present stance toward the problem. There is always something to advise; always another way to go. This is so because if the counselee were already doing what God says to do about the problem, and were sure of it, he would have had no need to come for counsel.

---

[3]The importance of using a modern translation is evident in passages like this one. Counselees, confused already by many things, do not need further complications added by the necessity for explaining KJV vocabulary like "charity."

The following case again illustrates the use of the Scriptures in an antithetical, confronting fashion, but from a slightly different perspective. Notice how a direct Word from God may be used to cut across false propaganda to give hope.

Check Up?

You dismissed Harry six weeks ago and set up a second check-up session after the first was canceled due to working overtime. Harry's wife called you an hour after the time of the appointment to notify you that he couldn't make it. Harry is a new Christian who has been trying to overcome drunkenness.

Harry is now sitting before you in tears confessing that he was drunk and that his problem is not solved as he had thought. "Maybe I can't stop drinking. Once a drunk always a drunk! I stayed away from all the places and people that you told me to. I even found three new ways home from work and alternate them. I guess I just don't love God enough." Harry sobbed.

"When did you get drunk and what was involved?" you inquire.

"I don't know exactly, but it began when my wife and I had an argument. She wanted to go out and I couldn't because I wanted to avoid the drinking at the club to which she wanted to go. She left anyway and I started feeling bad."

(Case II - 21, pp. 164,165)

Clearly, many things may be said about this case. But again, I wish to stress the use of the Scriptures in one respect only. People use language for two purposes: to speak to others, and to speak to themselves. They may not convince others readily, but they are usually very persuasive when talking to themselves! All of which is to say that the counselor should be aware of the damaging effects of frequently-repeated old sayings, cliches, proverbs (i.e., extra biblical proverbs), and the like.[4] Here, the statement "Once a drunk always a drunk" is a tragically false proverb that capsulizes a conviction of pagan despair. The counselor must see that Harry has become convinced that it is true. Perhaps this catch-phrase has been repeated again by him and by others. Possibly the conviction has been strengthened by statements of A.A. that support the contention. However he has reached this conclusion, you can be sure that it needs to be dislodged before real progress can be made. A man with the conviction (or even half-conviction) that there is no way to change once he has become a drunk will not have hope enough to endure the trials and the temptations that he must face. Here then, is the place for the counselor (who has also failed in other respects because he has not taught Harry according to Ephesians 4 and Colossians 3, and the significant verse in Ephesians 5:18, that drunkenness can only be removed by the two-factored process of putting on as well as putting off) to confront the concept packaged in the statement "Once a drunk always a drunk!" with the unequivocal word of the living God to the contrary. Turning to I Corinthians 6:11,12 he will read "drunkards" in the list of life dominating sins delineated, but also will continue to the end of the thought: ". . . such WERE some of you." Then he may comment: "God differs with your statement. He says that these Corinthian Christians had been able to put drunkenness behind them. Notice the past tense. By the grace of God you can do so too!" Harry needs to have his pagan notion challenged by the Scriptures.

[4]For more on this point, *The Christian Counselor's Manual*, pp. 103-116; 373.

Empathy

"My situation is so different," Laurie explained. Laurie, the wife of a young seminarian, had come (she said) because "I feel obligated to David to keep working, since I want him to be able to concentrate on school. I would never forgive myself if I quit my job, because he would have to reduce his class load in order to work, and I know that he wouldn't get as much out of school. But Pastor, I tell you, my job is impossible! I can't advance because I'm pegged as being temporary. I can't tell David or he'll tell me to quit. Less qualified men are promoted before me because, as my boss seemed happy to explain, 'a man's voice on the phone commands more respect, and therefore, is more valuable to the company.' And to top it off, I get no encouragement in the work that I am doing. I am losing my self-confidence; what shall I do?"

Laurie's story tugs at your heart; not long ago you and your wife were in nearly an identical situation. You can empathize with her and are inclined to advise her that she might change jobs at the earliest opportunity. But you are not sure; "Is there more that can be done for Laurie?" you wonder.

(Case I - 47, pp. 94,95)

In this case there are many features that might be emphasized. Let me quickly run through three. First, when Laurie says "My situation is so different" the counselor, properly identifying with her (not as he was tempted to in the *Casebook* account), might have referred to I Corinthians 10:13, quoting and explaining the verse,[5] and powerfully concluding with a reference to his own experience. In part, her despair and her evident self-pity

[5]Cf. *Christ and Your Problems.*

grew from her false, unbiblical notion that no one else had ever had to grapple with the difficulties with which she was struggling. The same verse also could be used to deal with her language (see previous case) which indicates that she has convinced herself that the situation is hopeless (cf. words of exaggeration: "never, impossible" and of impossibility: "can't," etc.). Secondly, I Peter 3 in general is appropos concerning her submission to her husband. She is already involved in a deception that could lead to serious marital communication problems. She first should have talked to him about her problem, and she should not have prejudged his reaction (in the actual case, he did not respond as she supposed). More specifically, by not telling him, she has made it difficult for him to exercise his responsibility to live with her "according to knowledge" (I Peter 3:7). She must be willing to reveal all such matters that deeply influence them jointly so that he can fulfill his obligation to understand her. Lastly, somewhere in this session, Laurie needs to be confronted with the biblical work ethic found at the end of the third chapter of Colossians. A Christian does not work for her boss' acclaim, nor merely for earthly rewards. "It is the Lord Christ" whom she serves. And it is the same Christ who will acknowledge her faithfulness: "Well done, you good, faithful servant."

It is possible to go on and on discussing other cases in like manner, but these should suffice to show how the Scriptures, used in counseling, guide the counselor as well as help him to guide the counselee. Each of the cases also may be examined according to the five essentials delineated at the beginning of Chapter II. As a further exercise, I suggest that you work your way through the *Casebook,* making a list of all of the pertinent passages of Scripture that might possibly be used in each case either as a guide to the counselor in dealing with the counselee or to the counselee in dealing with his problems. The list of passages in Chapter X will be found to be of valuable assistance in doing this.

CHAPTER X

Miscellaneous Comments About the Use of the Scriptures in Counseling

In this chapter I shall mention several important uses of the Scriptures in counseling. To begin with let me observe that the Scriptures should be used in homework assignments. I do not have time or space here to discuss either the place or use of homework in counseling. I have done so, however in several chapters in *The Christian Counselor's Manual* (q.v., if you are unfamiliar with the idea). However, I should like to emphasize here one aspect of homework that I have not discussed elsewhere: *how* the Scriptures may be used in homework.

It is important for the counselee himself to back up all counseling, and in particular, all of the work that he accomplishes through counseling, with prayer and the assimilation of Scripture. In every instance, the Christian counselee should be questioned about the regularity of his prayer and about his Bible study habits. Here I wish to speak about the latter. If he does not study the Scriptures daily, he should be encouraged to do so and given concrete help in doing so whenever necessary. One of the most helpful ways to promote daily Scripture study on the part of the counselee is to suggest that he begin by reading the Book of Proverbs (in a modern translation together with a good Bible commentary). In doing so, unless the first nine chapters are particularly pertinent to the problems that he is confronting in counseling, it is often wise to urge him to begin with the list of single proverbs that begins in chapter 11. In this way, he can read through slowly until he strikes a proverb that seems to embody a pithy concept that he needs to grasp and knead into the dough of his life. I usually advise him to stop whenever he has struck gold in this way. First, he should study the proverb to his satisfaction so that by help of his commentaries, Bible dictionaries and other reference works (whenever necessary), he understands the import of the proverb. He should spend at least an equal amount of time thinking about how the proverb applies to his life. He may need to turn it over again and again, looking at it from various angles. Or he may wish to write out (he will discover that forcing himself to write things out often is useful for assuring himself that he is not deceiving himself) the areas of his life to which the proverb applies and how. Each area, then, should be examined carefully to discover every implication. Whenever he follows this approach he should be quite specific (e.g., after reading Proverbs 12:25, he might make a notation in his study book:[1] "Bill is worried; I must give him an encouraging word from the Scriptures about his problem").

Next, let me point out a second use of the Scriptures. The Scriptures may be used in counseling to set and guide the course for some particular counseling task that must be performed. For example, whenever a conference table is set up in a home, we hand out the following form to the counselees. You will notice how it points to the reading of a particular portion of the Scriptures that directly pertains to the matter of Christian communication. Reading and rereading that portion at the outset of the conference reminds each party of God's requirements and

---

[1]Keeping a Study Book for recording results of studies preserves ideas for future use. The Book can be quite simply arranged with each page devoted to a passage. The page may be divided into two columns headed: Meaning of passage and Implications of passage for my life. The second column is essential if Bible Study is to become *telic* rather than merely oriented toward storage and retrieval.

thereby sets the tone of the conference and helps to cut down the counterproductive sinful attitudes, words and actions that previously were destroying good relationships between the participants.

SETTING UP A CONFERENCE TABLE

PLACE

Agree upon an area in which daily conferences may be held without interruption. Choose a table, preferably one that is not used frequently for other purposes. Hold all conferences there. If problems arise elsewhere, whenever possible wait until you reach home to discuss them—at the conference table, of course. The first week read Ephesians 4:17-32 each night before conferring.

Place_____

Time_____

PURPOSE

The conference table is a place to confer, not to argue. Begin by talking about yourself—your sins and failures—and settle all such matters first by asking forgiveness. Ask also for help (cf. Matthew 7:4-5).

Speak all the truth in love. Do not allow any concern to be carried over into the next day. Not all problems can be solved at one sitting. You may find it necessary to make up an agenda and schedule out the work over a period of time according to priorities. Direct all your energies toward defeating the problem, not toward the other person. Your goal is to reach biblical solutions, so always have Bibles on the table *and use them.* It helps to record the results of your work on paper. Open and close conferences with prayer. When you need help, reread Ephesians 4:25-32.

PROCEDURES

If any conferee argues, "clams up" or does anything other than confer at the table, the others must rise and stand quietly. This prearranged signal means, "In my opinion we've stopped conferring." Whether he was right or wrong in this judgment does not matter and ought not to be discussed at the moment. The person seated should then indicate his willingness to confer, and invite others to be seated again.

The conference table guide also points up the need for the counselees to use the Scriptures in order to reach solutions to problems. There are many ways in which people seek to solve life's questions. They may try to follow feelings or intuition, or act upon an experience. But Christian counselors will be zealous to teach counselees instead to rely upon the Bible. Therefore, as a part of their counseling they will make an effort at every appropriate point to stress the importance of consulting God's Word by giving assignments calculated to encourage and to help the counselee to learn to use the Scriptures profitably to deal with his life problems. Often this will entail instruction as to how to use the Bible practically, including directions about how to look for the *telic* emphasis of each passage. It may involve help about how to use dictionaries, commentaries, concordances and other Bible reference materials. The counselor, in each instance, must make an evaluation of the counselee's present capability to use the Scriptures effectively and not merely assume that an assignment to search the Bible for help in reaching a particular objective will be productive. The desire may be present to do so, but the counselee's lack of knowledge about how to go about the search may keep him from fulfilling that desire. Failure may further discourage him, and may confirm suspicions that the Bible is impractical.

One of the most important ends for counselors to pursue is understanding about *how to* find answers to life's questions in the Scriptures. Nothing will help counselees for the future more than this. Another factor in the use of the Scriptures is the importance of distinguishing between direct commands of God and valid inferences from and applications of such commands. Some matters are directly enjoined or forbidden; in others decisions must be made by inference from biblical principles. It is not necessary to spend time developing this theme here since in *The Christian Counselor's Manual* I have already done so.[2] Yet it is essential to stress the importance of making such distinctions. Otherwise, the counselee may fail to distinguish between the authority of God and the biblically-informed judgment of others. It is therefore significant when the counselor, in giving advice or in making an assignment himself makes such distinctions. Compare the following two statements: "Joe, you must stop running around with Bob's wife, and you must stop as of today!" and "Bill, you should study your Bible; I'd suggest that you might begin with the tenth chapter of Proverbs." The second differs radically from the first.

The distinction may be summarized in the following chart:

BIBLICAL COMMAND	COUNSELOR'S SUGGESTION
Outcome "Joe. . . you must stop"	Specific biblical steps for reaching it "Call her today"
General biblical principles "You must study your Bible"	Outcome "Read Proverbs 10 ff."

---

[2]Cf. pp. 16, 17, 447, 448.

The counselor may be very directive about commanding a certain outcome when the biblical commands directly govern it: "Joe you must stop running around with Bob's wife." When the case is not covered directly, one can be directive only about the principles that clearly are commanded: "You should study your Bible." It is not altogether certain biblically *how* Joe must put an end to his infidelity. Indeed, the steps that he takes to achieve this end may vary under different circumstances. If he can make a clean break with a phone call today, he should do so. If, however, Bob's wife keeps on trying to reestablish the relationship, that might call for different steps. On the other hand, studying the Scriptures regularly may be enjoined as a biblical principle, but the passages with which Bill begins can only be suggested. Circumstances again, might point to entirely different passages (e.g., if Bill is an unbeliever, he should probably not begin with Proverbs but rather with the Book of John).

In considering the various ways in which the Scriptures must be used by counselors, it is important to warn against moralistic, illustrational, prescriptional and abstract usage. A final word about each of these misusages of the Scriptures is in order.

Moralistic use of the Scriptures usually involves at least two faults. The first of these is a failure to show that the intended action must be done not merely to remove some grief or trouble from the counselee, but rather must be done primarily in order to please God. Secondly, the Scriptures are used moralistically when biblical principles or practices are enjoined in order to achieve a reformation apart from the saving work of Jesus Christ (both in justification and in the process of sanctification, which is the work of the Holy Spirit alone).[3]

[3]For counseling pamphlets that make a strong effort to overcome this problem, see my "What Do You Do When. . ." series (Presbyterian & Reformed Publ. Co., Nutley, N. J.: 1975).

Illustrational use of the Scriptures consists of proof-texting ideas set forth by you or someone else. The Scriptures often are used in an exemplary manner ("for instance, take the case of Daniel. . . ") to demonstrate some point that the counselor has made, a point that originally may have been taken from Rogers, Freud, Skinner, Harris, etc. The serious error involved in the illustrational use of the Scriptures is simply this: while one *sounds* scriptural, because he uses the Scriptures to back up his comments and ideas, in fact he is doing nothing more than that—using the Scriptures illustratively to BACK UP HIS OWN IDEAS. Instead, his ideas themselves must be gleaned from the Scriptures. Rather than illustrationally, the Scriptures should be used *foundationally.*

Prescriptional use of the Scriptures has already been mentioned at an earlier point in this volume, so I shall not say anything more about it here, except to remind you that the Scriptures cannot be given out to counselees as if they were a magic potion that (understood or not) will do him good. On the contrary, they must be explained and concretely applied to the specific problems that he confronts.

Abstract use of the Scriptures is closely related to the last error mentioned above. Setting forth principles and truths alone is often insufficient. The counselee usually does not know how to apply these to his life. While it is important to etch out principles so that these may be known and applied later in various circumstances, it is essential to show in the present one just *how* the principles work out. While it is true that a principle is the most practical element of all, it is also true that unless the counselee learns *how* to make principles practical by having someone *show* him *how* to do so, probably he will not find principles practical at all. Thus, the counselor, in this as well as in other things, will find himself again and again faced with the task of showing counselees *how to* use the Bible in a personal practical way.

All in all, there is nothing more satisfying than the proper use of the Scriptures in counseling because by such usage one does so many things at once. He helps by bringing God's sure Word to bear upon the counselee's problem. He honors God by pointing away from human wisdom to Him. He shows the counselee what a rich wealth of information is contained in the Bible, thus encouraging him to turn more often to this Source. And, he helps to instruct the counselee in the ways and means of using the Bible in days ahead for himself. Thus, by the use of the Scriptures, he helps solve problems now and prevents problems from reoccurring in the future.

CHAPTER XI
The Counselor's Topical Worklist

On the following pages, alphabetically arranged, there is a list of topics under each of which appears a limited number of selected Scripture passages. In many ways, this is a curious list, as a quick scanning will indicate. But, to counselors, the peculiar nature of the list is readily understandable and, indeed, constitutes its sole value. It is from beginning to end a counselor's list. It is a worklist, based upon many of the most commonly encountered areas of needs, sins and problems faced in the counseling context, together with references to key biblical passages that have proven particularly helpful in dealing with each of these topics.

Since the choice of the specific Scripture portions will vary from counselor to counselor, according to his understanding and even his interpretation of them, sufficient space has been provided beneath each entry for other references to be added. In this way, by making one's own additions, the list may become a valuable personalized reference source that may be used for many purposes, some of which may extend beyond counseling interests. Plainly, the list is limited but hopefully it is adequate. Too many topical or scriptural references would confuse the counselor who seeks to obtain quick help (perhaps at times even in the counseling session itself). Indeed, selectivity is what makes the list most useful. Since many persons have asked for just such a list, my expectation is that it will meet a real need.

Adultery
  Ex. 20:14
  II Sam. 11:2
  Prov. 2:16-18, 5:1-23,
  6:23-35; 7:5-27; 9:13-
  16
  Hosea, bk. of
  Mal. 2:13-16
  Mt. 5:28; 15:19; 19:9
  I Cor. 6:9-11

Alcoholism (See Drunk-enness)

Anger
  Gen. 4:5-7
  Psalm 7:11
  Prov. 14:17,29;
  15:1,18; 19:11,19;
  20:3,22; 22:24; 24:29;
  25:15,28; 29:11,22.
  Mark 3:5
  Eph. 4:26-32
  Jas. 1:19,20.

Anxiety (See Worry)

Associations (bad/good)
Prov. 9:6; 13:20; 14:9;
22:24; 23:20,21; 29:24
Rom. 16:17,18
I Cor. 5:9-13
II Cor. 6:14-18
II Tim. 3:5

Avoidance
Gen. 3:8
Prov. 18:1
I Tim. 6:11
II Tim. 2:22

Assurance
Hebrews 4:16; 6:11
I Peter 1:3-5
II Peter 1:10
I John 5:13,18,19

Bitterness (See Resentment)

Blame Shifting
Gen. 3:12,13
Prov. 19:3

Body
Romans 12:1,2
I Cor. 3:16,17; 6:18-20;
15
II Cor. 5:1-4

Children (See Family)

Church
Eph. 4:1-16
Heb. 10:25
Rev. 2,3

Change
Ezk. 36:25-27
Mt. 16:24
Eph. 4:17-32
Col. 3:1-14
I Thess. 1:9
II Tim. 3:17
Heb. 10:25
Jas. 1:14,15
I Peter 3:9

Commandment
Ex. 20
Prov. 13:13
Luke 17:3-10
John 13:34; 15:12
I John 5:2,3

Communication
Eph. 4:25-32

Conscience
Mk. 6:19
Acts 24:16
Rom. 2:15
I Cor. 8:10,12
I Tim. 1:5,19; 3:9
II Tim. 1:3
Heb. 13:18
I Peter 3:16,21

Confession
Prov. 28:13
Jas. 5:16
I John 1:9

Conviction
John 16:7-11
II Tim. 3:17
Jude 15

Death
Psalm 23:6
Prov. 3:21-26; 14:32
I Cor. 15:54-58
Philips. 1:21,23
Heb. 2:14,15

Desire
Gen. 3:6
Ex. 20:17
Prov.   10:3,24;   11:6;
  28:25
Mt. 6:21
Lk. 12:31-34
Rom. 13:14
Gal. 5:16
Eph. 2:3
Titus 2:12;3:3
Jas. 1:13-16; 4:2,3
I John 2:16
Jude 18
I Pe. 1:14; 4:2,3

Decision Making
II Tim. 3:15-18
Heb. 11:23-27

Depression
Gen. 4:6,7
Psalm 32,38,51
Prov. 18:14
II Cor. 4:8,9

Discipline
Prov. 3:11,12; 13:24;
19:18; 22:6,15; 23:13;
29:15
I Cor. 5:1-13; 11:29-34
II Cor. 2:1-11
Eph. 6:1-4
I Tim. 4:7
Heb. 12:7-11

Doubt
Jas. 1:6-8

Drunkenness
Prov. 20:1; 23:29-35;
31:4-6; 23:20
Eph. 5:18
I Pe. 4:4

Divorce
Gen. 2:24
Dt. 24:1-4
Isa. 50:1
Jer. 3:1
Mal. 2:16
Matt. 5:31,32; 19:3-8
Mk. 10:3-5
I Cor. 7:10-24,33-
34,39-40

Envy
Titus 3:3
Jas. 3:14-16
I Pe. 2:1

Family
Gen. 2:18,24
Ex. 20:12

Father (See Family)

Fear
Gen. 3:10
Prov. 10:24; 29:25
Mt. 10:26-31
II Tim. 1:7
Heb. 2:14,15
I Pe. 3:6,13,14
I John 4:18

Husband/Wife
Gen. 2:18,24
Eph. 5:22-33
Col. 3:18-21
I Pe. 3:1-17
I Tim. 2:11-15

Forgiveness
Prov. 17:9
Mt. 6:14,15; 18:15-17
Mk. 11:25
Lk. 17:3-10
Eph. 4:32
Col. 3:13
Jas. 5:15
I John 1:8-10

Parent/Child
Gen. 2:24
II Cor. 12:14
Eph. 6:1-4
I Tim. 3:4,5

Friendship
Prov. 27:6,10; 17:9,17
John 15:13-15

Grief
Prov. 14:13; 15:13
Eph. 4:30
I Thess. 4:13-18

Gifts
Rom. 12:3-8
I Cor. 12-14
I Pe. 4:10,11

Habit
Prov. 19:19
Isa. 1:10-17
Jer. 13:23; 22:21
Rom. 6-7
Gal. 5:16-21
I Tim.
Heb. 5:13ff.
I Pe. 2:14,19

Gossip
Prov.   10:18;   11:13;
18:8; 20:19; 26:20-22
Jas. 4:11

Homosexuality
Gen. 19
Lev. 18:22; 20:13
Rom. 1:26-32
I Cor. 6:9-11
I Tim. 1:10

Humility
Prov. 13:34; 15:33;
16:19; 22:4; 29:23
Gal. 6:1,2
Philips. 2:1-11
Jas. 4:6,10
I Pe. 5:6,7

Hope
Prov. 10:28; 13:12
Rom. 15:4,5
I Thess. 1:3; 4:13-18
Heb. 6:11,18,19

Jealousy (See Envy)

Laziness
Prov. 12:24,27; 13:4;
15:19; 18:9; 26:13-16
Mt. 25:26

Lying
Ex. 20:16
Prov. 12:19,22
Eph. 4:25
Col. 3:9

Love
Prov. 10:12; 17:19
Mt. 5:44; 22:39,40
Rom. 13:10
I Cor. 13
I Pe. 1:22
I John 4:10,19; 5:2,3
II John 5,6

Life-dominating Problems
I Cor. 6:9-12; 21:8
Eph. 5:18
Rev. 21:8; 22:15

Lust (See Desire)

Mother (See Family)

Obedience
I Sam. 15:22
Lk. 17:9,10
Acts 4:19; 5:29
Eph. 6:1
Heb. 5:8; 13:17
I Pe. 1:22

Listening
Prov. 5:1,2,13; 13:18;
15:31; 18:13

Peace
Prov. 3:1,2; 16:7
John 14:27
Rom. 5:1; 12:18; 14:19
Philips. 4:6-9
Col. 3:15
Heb. 12:14

Put off/Put on (See Change)

Reconciliation
Matt. 5:23,24; 18:15-17
Lk. 17:3-10

Pride
Prov. 8:13; 11:2; 13:10;
16:18; 18:12; 21:24;
27:1; 29:23

Repentance
Luke 3:8-14; 24:47
Acts 3:19; 5:31; 17:30;
26:20
II Cor. 7:10; 12:21

Resentment
Prov. 26:24-26
Heb. 12:15

Sexuality
Gen. 2:25
I Cor. 7:1-5

Reward/Punishment
Prov. 13:24; 22:15;
29:15
II Cor. 2:6; 10:6
Heb. 10:35; 11:26
II John 8

Shame
Gen. 2:25
Prov. 11:2; 13:18
I Cor. 4:14
I Pe. 3:16

Slander (See Gossip)

Stealing
Ex. 20:15
Prov. 20:10,22; 29:24;
30:7-9
Eph. 4:28

Worry
Prov. 12:25; 14:30;
17:22
Matt. 6:24-34
Philips. 4:6,7
I Pe. 5:6,7

Work
Gen. 2:5,15; 3:17-19
Prov. 14:23; 18:9; 21:5;
22:29; 24:27; 31:10-31
I Cor. 15:58
Col. 3:22-24
I Thess. 4:11
II Thess. 3:6-15

BOOKS BY JAY E. ADAMS

THE BIG UMBRELLA
CHRIST & YOUR PROBLEMS
CHRISTIAN COUNSELOR'S
    CASEBOOK
CHRISTIAN COUNSELOR'S MANUAL
CHRISTIAN LIVING IN THE HOME
COMPETENT TO COUNSEL
GODLINESS THROUGH DISCIPLINE
PULPIT SPEECH
SHEPHERDING GOD'S FLOCK I:
    PASTORAL LIFE
SHEPHERDING GOD'S FLOCK II:
    PASTORAL COUNSELING
THE USE OF THE SCRIPTURES IN
    COUNSELING
YOUR PLACE IN THE COUNSELING
    REVOLUTION
WHAT TO DO ABOUT WORRY